CAN YOUR BUSINESS STEP UP TO THE GROWTH CHALLENGE?

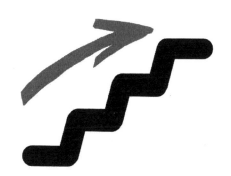

Ray Moore

Ray Moore UK

Copyright © by Ray Moore

All rights reserved. No part of this publication may be reproduced, stored in a retrieval system, or transmitted in any form or by any means, electronic, mechanical, photocopying, recording or otherwise, without prior permission of the author.

First Published 2013

For business people everywhere

Ray Moore

CONTENTS

■ ■ ■ ■

Foreword	7
Preface	9
Is This For You?	13
1. Introduction	17
2. Awareness	23
3. Moments of Clarity	29
4. The End in Mind	35
5. The Levels	43
6. Setting out the Stall	65
9. The Drivers	81
8. Structure	103
9. Mindset	145
10. Desire	167
11. Stop, Reflect and Review	183
Further help	189
Further Reading	193
About the Author	195

FOREWORD
■ ■ ■ ■

A superb book! There's no doubt Moore is a talented writer. This is a gripping and logical analysis of how to successfully grow a business. *The Levels* is an excellent work with wide appeal and is a must read for any business leader, manager, academic and ambitious business student. It should be a core text for today's business schools!

Throughout the book, Moore expertly examines the many challenges that businesses face in today's economy and distills them into an engaging and enjoyable read. Even more importantly, Moore provides the reader with clear, insightful and compelling answers to today's business problems. This book actually does what other books only claim to do and will become a definitive classic on how to effectively and sustainably grow a business.

Simon Daly, Director of Knowledge Transfer, Anglia Ruskin University

PREFACE

■ ■ ■

Over the years I have seen some businesses that have fantastic ideas, products or services that just get stuck, stop growing and fade away.

I have seen families and businesses ripped apart by feuds or those that have experienced the classic 'clogs to clogs in three generations' whereby the hard work of the original owner is lost in the process of succession. I have also seen many lovely business owners unable to retire because they are the business and know it will just fall apart if they were to leave. The examples go on and on. It is such a waste of potential, not only for the individuals involved, but also for the business community, economy and wider society.

On the other hand, I have seen some businesses and owners who have just done it. They have seen and exploited the potential their business has and created sustainable long-term wealth. Their business is exactly where they want it to be.

So what is the difference? For the last ten years, I have been striving to understand this better and help businesses achieve their potential.

While doing so, I came to realise the importance of the driving forces behind most businesses and identified the stumbling blocks that prevent many entrepreneurs from effectively growing their business. The Levels model was born!

This journey started for me soon after I successfully sold Alexander Industrial Supplies Ltd (AISEL) to Bunzl plc. in 2002 and has continued during my time as a business coach and advisor. The Levels model is in fact largely how I built up AISEL to a medium-sized company with healthy profits and readied it for sale. At the time, like many other business owners, I didn't realise exactly what I was doing and thought it was just common sense. Perhaps I am a slow learner or perhaps like so many things we often ignore the obvious.

So has this book been a labour of love over the last ten years? No way!

It has, however, been driven by the look in business owners' eyes when, as their coach, I've explained the Levels. It's the moment of realisation I see again and again. At last, someone has put into words what they are experiencing and the response is usually along the lines of "Yes, that is exactly where I am!" or "If only I had known this thirty years ago!"

So, the time is right for the Levels to be put under the spotlight. At its simplest, it is a manual for growth that focuses on the changes a business should put in place to make the difficult TRANSITION up from a small- to medium-sized company. At its most complex, it's a guide to challenging and changing your entire way of thinking!

The Levels model has been presented to audiences large and small hundreds of times. It has been discussed at length with a wide range of business professionals and has stood up to academic scrutiny. Most importantly, it has been successfully put into practice by growing businesses with fantastic results over the last ten years. So it works.

I hope you enjoy reading the book, but most of all I hope it enables you to change for the better and take your business to the place you want it to be. I would love to receive your feedback and, if you do find it useful, spread the word to other business owners because together we can unlock the potential of our economy for future generations.

Enjoy!

IS THIS FOR YOU?
■ ■ ■ ■

Type the words 'business growth books' into Amazon (or any similar site) and you'll get a staggering return of something like 54,000 results. Within this, you'll find everything from weighty *Financial Times* business guides to scientifically focused volumes on the language of management to your bulk standard 'get rich quick' guides.

If you're looking at seriously growing your business, it could be very easy to spend a small fortune buying endless copies of these books, only to find out that none of them is really helpful for you and your business.

Personally, I have no wish to waste anyone's time, so, let's get straight to the point and find out if this is the right book for you.

First of all, this book is aimed at anyone who is currently building or managing a Small to Medium Enterprise (SME).

In Chapter 5 we will look in more depth at this definition and its sub-categories but at the moment let's take it that this covers all businesses employing anything between one and 250 people.

That's a massive group! In fact, the latest statistics available (taken at the beginning of 2015) show there were some 5.4 million SMEs in the UK.

If your business is one of them, read on.

Secondly, this book is aimed at those of you who are starting to grow, or want to continue to expand, your business. Perhaps you have already achieved much of what you expected within your particular field and are now in a fairly comfortable position but have grown a little risk adverse. That's great if you're happy to stay in the comfy seat, but maybe you're experiencing a nagging feeling that you have not yet achieved everything you wanted to in your business, that your aim is to reach a bit further. If this is the case then keep reading.

Finally, if you and your business seem to have reached a bit of a plateau and, no matter how hard you work or how many hours you put in, you're struggling to break through to what you consider to be a bigger, higher level in your industry, then this book is also the right choice for you. If this is the case, your business is controlling you when surely it should be the other way round.

Basically, if none of this really applies, then stop reading right now, close this book and find something else to do with your time.

In case you're in any doubt, let's take a quick test.

Find somewhere quiet, away from any distractions, and ask yourself this question about your business and your future: In an ideal world, what kind of life do you envision and what is the size of your business?

Don't worry for a moment about how you are going to do it and all the reasons why it can't be done. If there were no restrictions and no fear of what the outcome might be, what would your business look like? Just get a picture in your head right now.... quick... before reality kicks in!

Now answer this: Is the vision of your life and business much bigger than what you have now?

If the answer is yes then this is definitely the book for you and welcome to the Levels!

Even if, at this moment, you believe your dream is way out of your reach or feel there are too many obstacles in the way then try to put those thoughts aside. This book will help you break them down.

Before we move on to actually looking at the Levels and the ways in which you can move closer to where your vision lies, let's get one thing clear: the vision you just created in your mind needs clarity to turn into a commercial reality.

Throughout this book, we'll be asking you to question every aspect of your business and challenge your way of thinking about it. The answers you come up with may not initially seem all that comfortable and, by the end, you may find that your idea of where you want to be is somewhat different from your original idea. Different or not, comfortable or not, what you will gain is a far greater understanding of what it is you actually want.

By the closing chapters of this book everything should start to seem very obvious.

That doesn't mean now is the time to jump straight to Chapter 11! Working through the Levels does require some work but the end result should be total clarity in your mind, a clear vision of the way forward and an understanding of the tools, techniques and resources you need to make that happen.

1
INTRODUCTION

In nature, if something is not growing or cannot adapt to changes in the environment it gradually starts to decay and eventually dies.

This also applies in business. The difference, of course, is that whereas in nature the seed sprouts a fledgling shoot and continues to grow steadily until it peaks by flowering, in business the path of growth is never a smooth straight line to the top.

For most SMEs, growth is the natural direction but they usually experience a pattern of growth followed by plateau, growth then plateau and so on – the path being more of a steep staircase than a smooth escalator ride. In addition, the business also sometimes experiences setbacks, when an attempt to reach the next step results in a nasty fall. This is usually when a period of growth has been launched into without proper planning, resulting in a business that cannot cope in its new environment or with its new structure and so returns to its previous plateau (a comfort zone).

So, how does a SME grow? What stages does it go through?

This is a question where you'll get multiple answers, depending on who you ask.

Academics tend to use terms like infancy, adolescence and maturity to describe the stages that a business enters. These are not bad descriptions as such but they tend to relate to the length of time the business has been going rather than its overall structure and ethos.

Companies House will categorise your business according to its turnover, balance sheet and number of employees and, with a little variation, EU definitions will do the same. Let's take another quick test. Look at the EU definitions below and place your business in one of those categories:

Micro – less than 10 employees with a turnover under *EUR 2 million (£1.3 million)*

Small – less than 50 employees with a turnover under *EUR 10 million (£6.25 million)*

Medium – less than 250 employees with a turnover under *EUR 50 million (£30 million)*

It was probably quite easy to find your company's position here, but what has it told you about where you are, other than the size and strength of sales? What does it tell you about growth? By these definitions, surely all you need to do to grow is employ more people and increase sales, right? Wrong!

THE LEVELS

Growth is something that is driven by many different factors but, in a nutshell, an enterprise will experience growth if it is well structured, employs the right variation of talent needed, offers the right products or services for the market and delivers these with great service. Even with all of these things in place, an enterprise cannot stop there. The final ingredient for continued growth is adaptability. Growth will always bring challenges and a business must change to benefit from new opportunities that arise.

Having worked with countless growing businesses across the wide SME spectrum, we've developed a model that charts their development. During the process of developing from a start-up position to a medium-sized company employing between 100-250 people, we found that most businesses experience four major plateaus. These are the Levels and unsurprisingly they are called Level 1, Level 2, Level 3 and Level 4.

Maybe not the most imaginative names, but we really don't want to distract from the power of this cycle with gimmicky names.

Looking purely at the number of people employed set out in the EU definitions and relating this to the Levels, Level 1 would be classed as micro, Levels 2 and 3 as Small and Level 4 as Medium. However, the point of the Levels model is to look in much more detail at the business – its size, its structure, the mindset of the business owner and his or her desires for the future as well as all the things that drive or restrict growth. There is also in fact a Level 0, but we'll go into that and much more detail about the nature and characteristics of each of these levels in Chapter 5.

All businesses grow at different speeds but the key to future growth and success is how quickly, upon reaching the plateau on one level, we can prepare to go to the next.

Let me explain a little more. There are four drivers that interact within every enterprise: Time, Team, Money and Delivery. We'll look at each of these drivers and how they can be properly managed later in this book but the main point to remember is it's all about balance. On reaching any of the levels (the plateau) all four drivers are in balance. Growth places pressure on these four drivers and forces them out of balance but, importantly, for a business to continue to grow profitably over the long term, these drivers need to be managed to remain in balance through the growth cycle as well as the plateau cycle.

Let's look at the impact of the drivers on the growth of a business by way of a simple example:

A business grows naturally and reaches a point where it is just starting to rise beyond Level 2. At this point, more opportunities are coming into the business's path and there is a need for more people to cope (Team). However, the business owner is just too busy dealing with enquiries to worry about recruiting (Time) so things get missed and, as well as not being able to take proper advantage of all the new opportunities, existing customers are let down (Delivery). This leads to complaints and then cash comes under pressure (Money). Sales fall and the business rebalances again at Level 2 as growth becomes naturally restricted.

The step up is just too steep and the business seems to have no option but to retreat back down to the level below.

Every time the business grows, the same pressure points build up with the same outcome – an imbalance that causes the business to struggle significantly in terms of cash flow and service delivery. There may be a different combination of events but the end result is the same. The business returns to Level 2. It's a similar situation to playing a game of snakes and ladders where you struggle square by square to the top, only to hit a giant snake two spaces from the end.

At this point though, the business makes more money, cash flow is brought under control and customers are happy once again. Where is the business owner in all of this? Right back to working what they see as long but acceptable hours.

However, overall growth stalls and the business cannot evolve beyond Level 2. Indeed, this has become its Business Comfort Zone (BCZ) and eventually the safe level at which the business can profitably operate. The business owner may well become unknowingly risk adverse and believe that Level 2 is the limit for the business to grow. At this point they put their dreams to one side and accept the situation.

Perhaps, the seeds of a slow and lingering death for the business have been sown.

So, where did they go wrong?

Whilst we've used this as an example, it is in fact an all too common situation that we especially see in businesses aiming to jump the hurdle from Level 2 to 3. The problem basically arises from the fact that, while developing into an organisation of around fifteen people (Level 2), most businesses grow quite naturally through the simple hard work, stamina and determination of the business owner. It works until that point, but the TRANSITION to the next level requires much greater thought about the resources needed, substantial structural and leadership changes and a major shift in the mindset of the business owner. It's what I call 'Setting out the Stall' – giving recognition to and planning for change before it actually happens and before the full impact is felt on your business.

2
AWARENESS

Before we move on to more detail about the Levels, I want you to take a moment to consider something very basic about yourself as a business owner and about your business.

I could guarantee that if we took a look at either your personal or company CV, it would be full of scenarios that demonstrate your admirable levels of knowledge, experience and skills. But, how often do you really look at any of this and truly assess what you learned and understood from any of these experiences? The question is one of awareness.

Knowledge or experience without true understanding is worthless.

My job here is not only to explain how the Levels model works and applies to business growth, but also to make you aware of the impact the Levels is having on your business. Whilst reading this book, it's your job not only to know what the Levels are but also to seek to understand them. By passing on the understanding rather than just the knowledge, I hope to help you get into a position where you can effectively use the Levels to your advantage when building your business.

OK, so let's look at how awareness impacts on your business.

Would you agree that in business plenty of opportunities exist?

If your answer is 'no' here, then I can only assume you've shut yourself away in a windowless office for the past few years. Yes, there are times when the economy takes a battering and the market is tough, but in reality we are still surrounded by a limitless number of opportunities.

The trouble is we are often not aware of them and even if we can see the opportunity we are unable to take advantage of it.

I once saw a famous illusionist/mentalist perform an experiment on a number of people, some of whom considered themselves to be lucky while others saw themselves as unlucky. The purpose of this experiment was to prove that 'luck' had nothing to do with it. It was in fact all about whether the people in question were aware of the opportunities around them and whether they were bold enough to take them. In one instance, the illusionist placed a £50 note right on the doorstep of a man claiming to be very unlucky to see what would happen. Of course, he came out in the morning and stepped right over it!

I want you to really see how awareness impacts on your business so let's look at it another way ...

THE LEVELS

In Figure 1 the crosses represent the opportunities around you. You will notice at the bottom of this box, there are a handful of opportunities bound by the knowledge you've gained through experience.

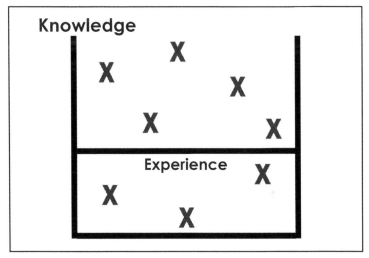

Fig 1

These are the opportunities that you are aware of and therefore can exploit. However, all those above that box are outside of your awareness and understanding and therefore beyond your ability to exploit.

Wouldn't it be great to expand that box?

But hang on a moment. If the area bound by experience took us ten, twenty or thirty years to accumulate, how long is it going to take to expand that area? Putting it another way, perhaps our experience is restricting our ability to exploit opportunities.

I am not saying that by reading this book you will instantly gain the knowledge and understanding you need to raise that experience line and therefore have easy access to more opportunities... if only it were that simple! It is going to take some work from you. Try this quick test to get your started:

Ask yourself the following two questions and give yourself a score between 0 and 10, with 0 being at the extreme 'not at all' and 10 being at the extreme 'very much' end of the spectrum.

1. How happy are you to learn?
2. How happy are you to change?

Be totally honest with yourself here and then multiply the two numbers together. Is it 100? Is it in the seventies? Maybe your result is closer to sixty. If you're starting to worry that your answer is even lower, don't! In fact, when we've asked business owners to take this test, the majority have come back with an answer somewhere in the forties. What's also interesting is that, in most cases, the answer to the first question is higher than the answer to the second. But, what is the point of being prepared to learn if you're not equally prepared to change?

Remember the old adage "If you always do what you always did, you will always get what you always got". Trite but true.

THE LEVELS

I want you to think of this as you read this book. The Levels model will make you more aware of what has happened or is happening in your business right now. Your role is to constantly review your experience to date.

After each of the following chapters, my challenge to you is to Stop, Reflect and Review. Write down your experiences so far, how the topic covered in the chapter relates to your business and what steps you can take to make a change.

Even if there are chapters or sections you don't really agree with, still take the time to review. It is the act of considering the Levels model that will make you aware of what is driving your business.

So, the first step is learning how to review and becoming aware that you may need to change the way you do things if you want to move forward and grow.

When you take a good look at your experience to date you may be in for a surprise. Maybe the CV says forty years' experience in a particular field. Interestingly, what we think of as forty years' experience gained in the cut and thrust of business can actually be only five years' experience that has been repeated over and over again. It just gets photocopied in each successive year.

Looking back at Figure 1 briefly, by truly understanding your experience and how you have arrived at where you are now, you will be in a position to expand the area under that experience line and as it expands you will become aware of many more opportunities that you will be able to exploit in the near future.

Indeed, it will allow you to think and act outside the box. Sorry if you saw that one coming!

The next step is then passing on that understanding to your team so that you can really take control of that expanded area and maximise the opportunities. This would also be a time to look at the idea of recruiting team members who may actually have more knowledge or experience than you, the business owner. A scary thought, huh? But don't worry, it doesn't have to be awkward or painful.

Before we move onto the Levels (yes we are getting there) let's just take a moment to look at the importance of reviewing your experiences.

3
MOMENTS OF CLARITY
■ ■ ■ ■ ■

When we think about experience it's as if we are building a wall with each additional experience adding another brick. We build brick upon brick and continue in this way until we've created layers (or years) of experience.

Now, as the wall rises, what is important to note is that the experience at the base level (the early years) ends up supporting all the similar experiences that come further up (the later years).

On its own this isn't a problem. If the very first experience (the single base brick) was fully understood then, for a while at least, it will be strong enough to support the rest.

However, if we didn't truly understand a particular experience, that bottom brick now supports two related bricks in the next layer, which in turn supports three related bricks in the next layer and so on. The result is something that looks like a precarious upside-down pyramid. (See Figure 2)

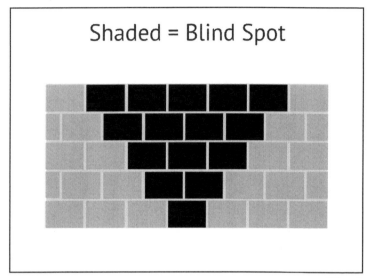

Fig 2

By the fifth layer that one brick is supporting fourteen related bricks. So that one occurrence that we did not understand now causes a huge blind area in our experience. Believe me, if left to continue the resulting effect could be disastrous – the wall will soon start to show cracks and could easily come tumbling down.

These blind areas are those we find difficult to explain to someone else. We can show them how to do something but when questioned further about the experience or task, we cannot see why the other person just doesn't get it. To us, it seems like 'common sense' and our frustration might well leave us thinking the other person is perhaps 'just a bit thick'! However, the real problem lies in the

THE LEVELS

blind areas. Because we don't really understand what we do, we can't get someone else to do it and so we're destined to do the task forever.

Let's look at an example of this in action. Imagine a growing bricklaying company employing over 100 bricklayers. One business owner (Joe) takes responsibility for sales and the other (Jack) takes responsibility for managing the sites.

As the business grows, the number of sites increases but Jack feels he cannot delegate his quality checking role to his site foremen. They constantly miss things that Jack sees as common sense. It soon gets to the point where Jack is running around trying to keep on top of the sites when he actually has some very capable people who could be helping him. Jack becomes a bottleneck and it's not long before clients start complaining about the delays.

When Jack is asked how he knows whether a piece of work (say a wall) is good or not, his reply is he "just did". With a quick look he can easily tell if it is right based on his thirty years of experience in the building industry.

However, after some further gentle questioning, Jack realises that, in that single moment of looking at the wall, he is unconsciously asking himself fifteen questions or more. When he finally took the time to understand what those questions were, it became easy to write them down and systemise the process of quality checking so that the foremen could carry out the task, freeing up Jack's time.

Whenever these blind areas arise, the same thought processes are applicable for all business owners. Only by truly seeking to understand and develop our awareness can we suddenly understand that first supporting brick and, in fact, understand all fifteen bricks.

It's that moment of clarity that will help you make the change.

But, how does this happen?

Well, sometimes it goes like this....

Pow!

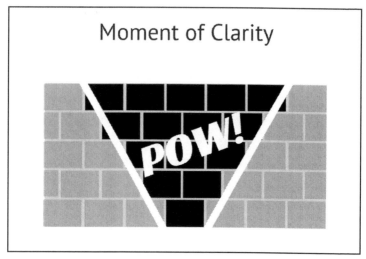

Fig 3

We have a moment of clarity, when understanding dawns upon us. It suddenly seems so obvious and we wonder why we couldn't see it before. The proverbial pink elephant is standing right there in front of us!

The problem here is that such moments of clarity can come along at any odd time.

Sometimes they just pop into our mind when we are busy doing something totally unrelated or they may wake us up in the middle of the night and for a split second it is so clear.

Annoyingly, they make their way into our head when we are not ready for them and, because we are busy on another task or want to get back to sleep, they just pop straight out of our head again. The moment of clarity itself is great news but the inability to action it means those fifteen bricks are still in the blind zone.

This is where the importance of Review becomes clear.

Taking time out to focus on each actual experience, what it has been built upon and what it supports within your business, is the only way to turn a moment of clarity into the commercial reality of being able to take advantage of more opportunities.

Put your reviewing techniques into action right now and try this.

Think back to when you first started your business. Without doubt there were areas of business you didn't quite understand or know how to deal with at the time. Take one of these experiences and consider what your misunderstanding was. Has it ever been rectified? Or have you just built layers on top of it?

OK, now think back to all the moments of clarity you've had over the years. How many of them have ever led to action or change? What is the commercial impact of all those ignored insights?

It's frightening isn't it? But don't worry, by thinking these things through you've already started to make a change and already increased your business's chances of advancing through the Levels.

4
THE END IN MIND

You may recall that at the very beginning of this book, I asked you to consider a question:

In an ideal world, what life do you envision and what is the size of your business?

It's a big question so let me put it to you again but more simply:

What do you want in life?

Now, don't panic. We're not about to get all philosophical and start a discussion on the meaning of life, the universe and everything!

This is a book about how to grow your business and, in actual fact, this really is the sixty-four thousand dollar question. It's the one that gives meaning and purpose to everything.

If you're having problems coming up with an answer, don't worry. You are in good company as, from my experience, most business owners can't answer this simple question either. Most of the time they are just too caught up in the daily 'doing' and don't have time to consider the end goal. Sometimes, they just forget the reason why they ever started doing what they are doing in the first place!

Consider this situation for a moment.

Imagine, you are walking down a road and you notice there is a bricklayer working across the street. He is busy building a wall and, as you draw closer, you notice how he is laying the bricks in a steady methodical way. Each layer is perfect and the colour of the mortar is consistent. It looks wonderful and you just know he is a true craftsman.

Fascinated by how he works, you stop and watch for a while, curious as to what it is he is actually building. Intrigued, you decide to cross the road and ask:

"I hope you don't mind me asking, but I am so impressed at what you are doing. Can you tell me what are you building?"

At which point, the bricklayer stops, puts down his trowel, smiles and says:

"Sorry, I don't have a clue. I come here every day and work hard. I'm just getting on with building – brick by brick!"

Now, your first thoughts about the bricklayer are probably something along the lines of "Is he crazy? Here he is working hard every day, putting all his craftsmanship into practice but has no idea what he is building. What a waste of time!"

Sounds a bit daft, doesn't it? But how many business owners truly know what they are trying to build? Wouldn't it be better to start out with a clear idea of what it is going to be like when it is finished?

Interestingly, there are three types of bricklayers.

The first are those that are simply happy putting one layer of bricks onto the previous, brick by brick. Doing high quality work fast and efficiently is their byword. They work hard and focus on the task in hand.

Then there are those that are looking to know how much they are earning per hour, what their take home pay is going to be and how long they have until they can put their tools down. They are just on the job treadmill with no time to do anything else. They exchange their time for money and, as long as at there is something in the bank at the end of the week, then all is well.

And lastly, there is the bricklayer who has a clear idea of what they are building. They have seen the plans and know how big the structure will be, how many floors will be built, what will support it, what the finishing touches will be and much, much more.

This is a person who inspires and motivates others to help them in order to complete the build.

People are drawn to help them and ultimately they achieve their dream.

As business owners, aren't we just like one of these bricklayers? Which one describes you the best?

Unfortunately, we have found that most business owners are often stuck in type one or type two bricklayer modes. They forget or indeed lose sight of what the final building is going to look like.

It might be reasonable at this point to ask what the problem is. If they're getting the job done, does it matter?

Well, yes it does!

Look at the bricklayer we met in the street again. Aside from putting one brick on top of another, at some point he also has to call upon a number of other professionals for advice – the structural engineer, the architect and the banker to name just three. As the bricklayer doesn't know what he is trying to build, all of these professionals will form their own view on what he is trying to achieve.

The structural engineer may think he is building a bungalow, the architect may think he is building a palace and the banker may think he is building an office block. Extreme examples but hopefully you get my drift.

Each professional gives the best advice they can but it is based on what they believe the bricklayer is building. Is it any wonder that the final building ends up looking like the 'House that Jack Built'.

It is nothing like what it started out to be, it's not watertight and has subsidence. It will only be with a great deal of luck that the roof won't fall in!

OK, so let's get back to your business.

You may have a number of employees and advisers at your disposal ... sales people, administrators, an accountant, lawyer, banker, financial advisor and perhaps a business coach. What would happen if you and your whole team of employees and advisers truly understood what you are trying to build?

So, I ask you once again to think about what you want your life to be like.

Don't worry how you are going to get there and ignore all doubts that it will never happen. Put aside also all of your friends and family's freely given advice. While well meaning, it is rarely helpful. The vision must come from you.

Take a moment to dream your future. Once you have that clear vision of what you want your life to be like, the next step is to work out how much cash flow you would need to maintain that lifestyle. Don't forget that the cash flow must be passive, meaning it cannot be so reliant on you to produce it that it hinders you from living your imagined future lifestyle. Basically, the business has to be able to run and be profitable without you there.

So here comes the quantum leap. The question of what you want in life suddenly becomes lots of questions about your business.

What does your future lifestyle look like?

What does your business look like to support that future?

How big does it need to be to produce the necessary cash flow?

What will be the approximate value of your business?

How can you get your business to a position where it doesn't rely on you?

And, most importantly, how well do you and your team understand the end goal?

Having a clearly defined end goal for your business brings so many benefits. With total clarity you can align everything in your business to that goal and this in itself is a very attractive and motivating position for your team. A clear vision will attract the right people to your business.

Always keeping the end in mind, I want you to consider where your business is now compared to that goal.

Think of your ultimate potential level as a score of 10 (where the end goal has almost entirely been achieved) and now give yourself a performance level between 0-10 (where you are now).

When asked to do this, we find that on average companies rate their performance at 4. This means there is a gap of 6, the interfering elements that sit in between ultimate potential and current performance. In fact we can write it as an equation:

**Current Performance
= Potential −
Interferences**

Now ask yourself, What are these interfering factors? What is it that is stopping your performance from being higher? You'll probably come up with a long list (time, resources, confidence, experience, money and so on) but crucially most of the interference is actually coming from the mindset of the business owner – YOU!

Often we strive to improve our current performance without dealing with (or even recognising) those things that are stopping us from achieving our potential. By removing or reducing the interferences, your performance can be greatly improved, meaning you can move much closer towards your full potential. The only thing stopping you is you!

It may not be the most comfortable position to be in or the biggest boost to your ego but accept it. The way you think about your business is likely to be the primary factor in holding it back.

Understanding how to make radical mindset changes is something we'll look at in more detail in Chapter 9 but what I hope is that, by now, you're already starting to arrive at some of the answers you need to drive your business into growth.

To recap, think over these questions once more:

- Do you want to expand your business?

- What size is your business currently at and where do you want it to be?

- Do you feel you've reached a comfort zone where everything is ticking over nicely but not growing any further?

- As the owner, what kind of hours are you putting in? Are you happy to continue this? Do you feel your business is controlling you?

- Do you feel you are missing opportunities? What is stopping you from taking advantage of them?

- How willing are you to change your way of thinking and doing?

- What kind of bricklayer are you? Do you know what you are building? Is the end goal clear to you and to everyone else around you?

5
THE LEVELS

Having dealt with the big questions of what you want out of life and how you want your business to grow, it's now time to take a more thorough look at the Levels themselves and what actually happens when a business makes the TRANSITION from one level to the next.

Not all enterprises will grow through all the levels. As you read more, it is important to keep this in mind. There are in fact many successful businesses that simply sit very comfortably at their current level. The key point about them is that the four drivers that interact with all businesses (remember Time, Team, Money and Delivery) are all in balance.

An equilibrium has been reached and the business owner is satisfied with that.

Other businesses will not move through the levels due to constraints placed upon them by the business owner, the market or the economy. However, the worst-case scenario is where a business is aiming for growth but gets stuck between the levels and cannot manage the pressures on each of the four drivers, which are then forced out of balance.

The most likely result here is poor profitability, strained cash flow, a demotivated and stressed team and probably some much damaged customer relationships.

Often in these cases, it is one of these underlying constraints i.e. the market movement, economy conditions or sometimes a positive business decision by the owner, that pushes the business back to the previous level, where balance is restored. This results in a return of profitability, much improved cash flow, reduced pressure on the team and restored customer relationships. If the owner is still aiming for growth but makes no significant changes in their business, this cycle can be repeated over and over again.

As a business coach, over the years I have interviewed many business owners who had once built their company to a much larger entity than its current size. They then shrunk the business (often referred to as "consolidated"), relieved the pressure and returned to a Business Comfort Zone (BCZ). They might refer to this as the best thing that ever happened. But consider this: during this time, they had also become risk adverse, had entirely abandoned their previous ambitions (the end goal) and were now continuing along the well trodden road of being heavily involved in the day-to-day running of their business. Was it really the best thing that ever happened?

This is the Levels in action and it affects SMEs across the board.

By recognising the constraints, the issues around imbalance and their symptoms within your business, you can use the Levels to your advantage.

5.1 Definitions and Statistics

OK, so definitions and statistics might not be the most exciting thing to think about but try not to fall asleep here as there are points to be learned. I have mentioned the term SME quite a lot so far but, to properly understand the Levels in action, it really needs a little bit of context.

The SME market is considered one of the major drivers of the economy. However, it is commonly referred to in very generic terms and often sweeping statements are made about SMEs without necessarily understanding the needs of the different segments within that market. Listen to any mainstream business editor from the world of broadcasting and you'll soon see what I mean about sweeping statements.

Oddly, although the SME tag covers a huge range of businesses, there doesn't appear to be any kind of universal definition. The government has its version; banks have another and the multitude of business training providers no doubt have a multitude of definitions to match.

For the purpose of keeping things simple and retaining a little of my own personal sanity, I have gone to the EU to get this definition, which we'll use here:

Micro, small and medium-sized enterprises are defined according to their staff headcount and turnover or annual balance-sheet total.

A medium-sized enterprise is defined as an enterprise which employs fewer than 250 persons and whose annual turnover does not exceed EUR 50 million (£30 million) or whose annual balance-sheet total does not exceed EUR 43 million (£27 million).

A small enterprise is defined as an enterprise which employs fewer than 50 persons and whose annual turnover and/or annual balance sheet total does not exceed EUR 10 million (£6.25 million)

A micro enterprise is defined as an enterprise which employs fewer than 10 persons and whose annual turnover and/or annual balance sheet total does not exceed EUR 2 million (£1.3 million)

Now be honest, did you just see loads of figures there and skip straight over them? If you did, go back and have another look because I want you to see how real people running real businesses across the UK fit into these definitions.

In the UK in 2015, there are some 5.4 million businesses that are defined as SMEs by the

Statistical Office. You might think that, as a key driver of the economy, most of these are employing a reasonable number of people and exhibiting pretty healthy balance sheets. Wrong!

What's interesting is that seventy-six per cent, or 4.1 million, of these enterprises do not employ any staff. In effect they are operating as sole traders and should be considered as self-employed jobs rather than a 'business'. This is a group that does not sit within the Levels of business growth. They are in fact at Level 0 (see more on this in section 5.2).

Based on the EU employee (definitions above), of the remaining 1.3 million businesses eighty-three per cent (1.1 million) are micro enterprises, fifteen per cent (204000) are small enterprises and only two per cent (33000) are medium sized enterprises.

Perhaps not quite what we expected?

The reality is that the SME market is extremely diverse, the demands of these three segments are completely different and the complexity of business growth from micro to small to medium brings totally different issues.

5.2 Size and Behaviour

"Size isn't everything!"

It may be a cliché but, actually when it comes to the Levels, you'll see it's not only the size of the business that matters. Factors such as how the business is structured and behaves along with the mindset of the owner are crucial.

Let's take some time here to have a look at the Levels Model (Figure 4). "At last!" I hear you say. It's just over the page. I hope you're excited to see it ...

Fig 4

Now, notice some of the structural areas a business will need to look at throughout the process of growth (those in the centre) and the mindset changes (those on the right). What we're talking about here is developing the foundations of your business, your team, your marketing and so on but also developing your mindset from that of a 'do-er' on the job to a leader. We'll come back to this in chapters 8 and 9 but, for now, let's think more about how a business behaves at each of these levels.

Level 0 – The Day Tripper Phase

At Level 0, we have the huge amount of self-employed individuals and fledgling start-ups.

It is here that we find the many who refer to themselves as 'one man bands' but I actually prefer the term 'one man armies'! After all, these are people who are pretty much managing every aspect of their work themselves – selling, doing, invoicing, accounting and so on. The boundaries between their work and home life are completely blurred, and within the wide ocean of business opportunities, they are similar to the kind of boats you see moored at the quayside announcing an array of day trip opportunities. Every day begins with a 'to do' list and the search for new customers. Every day ends with a cash count and maintenance check.

Capacity is the overriding issue for anybody working at Level 0. Every day, the boat has to scramble among the competition to gain enough customers to give the owner an income but, if too many customers turn up there simply aren't enough seats. Disappointed customers then look elsewhere (at the many other similar excursions on offer around them) and reputation and cash flow for the business owner is adversely affected. So begins a very familiar cycle of feast/famine.

Level 1 – The Power Boat Phase

At Level 1, we find the micro companies employing on average five to ten people. In many cases their turnover is a lot less than the £1.3m stated in the EU definition above!

Micro businesses behave like a powerboat. They are nippy, manoeuvrable and flexible, all of which gives them a great advantage in beating other boats to the action. Their costs are low so they can offer low prices and still make a living but that can often undermine a market. Because they are close to the sea, they can easily see all the things coming their way and react quickly. However, this also means they have to really focus on the moment. If the skipper (business owner) takes their hands off the controls for an instant, disaster can ensue.

The skipper is the one who fixes the engine, maintains the boat, makes sure they have the right crew, is constantly on the lookout for the next job and gets stuck in whenever they arrive at that job.

The pitfalls they face come directly from the choppy or stormy conditions of the ocean. For one thing, they are surrounded by other powerboats (the competition) and the constant race to every job results in the boat and its crew taking a real pounding. There's never enough time to properly maintain and improve the boat or develop the team and while slowing down might make the ride a little more comfortable, it certainly doesn't help them win any trophies.

In reality, what this means is that many businesses reach Level 1 and stay there. The emphasis is on sales, there is a high demand for their goods or service but they can't follow through on delivery. This of course leads to loss of sales and loss of money. Do you see how the four drivers are interacting here? The process of slowing down brings the business back down to its plateau and puts these back in balance and so begins a bumpy ride that takes them up and down that plateau but never enables them to reach as far as the next level.

Level 2 – The Fishing Boat Phase

Employing less than fifty (but more likely around fifteen) people, small businesses behave more like a fishing boat, the sort that battles the storms of the North Sea. It's built to weather the conditions but it relies very heavily upon the skill and knowledge of the skipper (owner) to keep it safe.

From hard-earned experience, the skipper knows where the fish are most likely to be and keeps a close eye on the weather. The skipper doesn't have to get stuck in hauling the nets or sorting and storing the catch. The crew take care of that. So, what does the skipper do all day?

The skipper works long, hard hours to ensure the boat and crew are safe as well as locating the right catch to feed everyone on the boat. The boat itself is built strong enough to face most conditions but will often have to trudge back to dock to face long and expensive repairs. Some of the catch (the past profits) must be pumped back into the boat just to keep it afloat.

The three main danger zones here are:

If the condition of the boat is not kept up to scratch then the stormy sea will claim it.

The boat can easily become top heavy (with too many overheads) and capsize.

Without the skipper, the boat would drift and eventually sink.

In other words, the business is too reliant on the owner who works from their gut and is guided by their experience. In this way, they are keeping every aspect of the business within their control but what they do cannot be easily taught, making it very difficult to start the handover process needed to take the business to Level 3.

Right now, the owner may have a fairly good income and lifestyle but the crux of it is they are extremely time-poor and there is no real value in the business itself. Without the owner and his or her years of hard graft, it would be virtually worthless.

Level 3 – The Cruise Liner Stage

At Level 3, a medium-sized business is probably employing somewhere in between fifty and 100 people and navigating the ocean in a vessel that operates more like a cruise liner.

The captain spends some of his time on the bridge but he doesn't have to be there all the time. The senior members of the crew (a management team) can competently man the bridge whilst the captain spends some time with the passengers (customers) and the rest of the crew (the wider team).

The safety and progress of the ship is the captain's main responsibility so they need to rely upon their various teams to handle their tasks with considerable autonomy and keep them abreast of any relevant information they need to make informed decisions.

So, on board we have the communications crew (accounts and administration) who are constantly checking the depth of water under the ship and that the ship stays on course. The wireless section (marketing) is monitoring what is going on around the ship and getting all the weather updates. The purser department (customer service) ensures the passengers are happy and informed about what's going on. The entertainment department (sales team) is down in the bar or in the Jacuzzi schmoozing the passengers! Only joking... unless it's after 3pm of course!

The liner itself is large enough and built with stabilisers to face large swells in the ocean with ease and also can survive major storms relatively untouched.

It's only here (at Level 3) that the captain does not have to be the business owner. Putting a new captain at the helm of the liner is much easier than replacing the skipper in a small boat. With the right team in place, the business is basically no longer reliant on the owner and his/her past experience.

The captain (perhaps a general manager) will ensure the boat continues on its chartered course with all the crew knowing where they are headed and their role and responsibilities in reaching the planned destination.

The business owner meanwhile has the freedom to be onshore if they so desire. They keep a check on the condition of the ship, its crew and passengers at all times and always know where the ship is headed and whether it is on course. However, they can do all of this from onshore, knowing the ship is in good hands.

Level 4 – The Fleet

At Level 4, we find the minority of businesses that are either at the larger end of the medium-sized company definition (with 100-250 employees) or those on the verge of becoming a much larger corporation.

As the business grows from Level 3 to 4, it becomes less of a major transformation than a process of replication. The business at this stage behaves like a fleet. Everything that has been achieved to get the business to the cruise liner stage is simply multiplied.

Now a fleet of liners, the business has huge momentum and becomes more immune to the state and conditions of the sea. Collectively, they carry plenty of mass and so can plough through stormy weather without missing a beat.

The owner may make an appearance on board one of the liners now and then, but by and large they remain on shore, take a back seat and spend far more time on the tropical islands the liners pass by than within the bows of one of their ships.

Where such businesses can become a little unstuck is when any kind of change of direction is required. With so many liners to keep track of, corrections to the steering of an entire fleet can take a long time. However, it can usually get to where it wants to be eventually and the business at this stage rarely takes a plunge to the seabed. It's a good job too as if it does, the repercussions can be widely damaging to the entire ocean. Indeed the situation can often need society and/or government support to help with the clear up.

5.3 Transition

I'm willing to guess that by now you've got a picture of yourself in mind wearing a skipper's hat, hands sturdy on the wheel, shouting out orders about port or starboard side. No? Oh, well maybe that's just me!

Fantasy lifestyles aside, now that you are more aware of where your business sits in terms of its size and behaviour, the question is how do you set about moving onwards and upwards? How do you get through the TRANSITION process from one level to the next while keeping the business in balance?

Remember, when the four main drivers of business (Time, Team, Money and Delivery) are out of balance, your business will not be able to face the challenge of growth successfully.

Time for another quick test. Consider both your business and personal life for a moment and then answer each of the following questions:

- When was the last time you took a holiday?

- How frequently were you able to fully 'switch off' from work while away? (Be honest here!)

- How often do you feel there are not enough hours in the day?

- How often do you work from home in the evening or on weekends?

- How much of your time do you set aside purely for family or other leisure activities?

- Why do you keep hold of many of your daily tasks instead of delegating them to others?

- How would you rate your business in terms of staff morale, stress and initiative?

- How often do you feel stressed or under pressure?
- How healthy is the company's record in terms of profitability, cash flow, margins and delivery?
- How rare or frequent are customer complaints?

Your answers will give you a good indication of whether your business is sitting on a balanced plateau or attempting to grow through a TRANSITION period and experiencing some of the most common out-of-balance symptoms. I hope this is pretty self-explanatory but basically, if your answers feel negative (e.g. you can't switch off on holiday, you don't have enough hours in the day and so on) then you're experiencing an imbalance.

So, how does anyone ever take their business through this growth period?

Interestingly, there are a great number of organisations set up to help the micro and small businesses get off the ground from government bodies such as universities and Business Link to the Federation of Small Businesses, banks, accountants and coaches of all shades. For the businesses that achieve medium size there is the CBI, IOD, business schools and so on.

However, I've found there is very little help, or indeed books, for businesses going through the small/medium TRANSITION phase. It's incredible really because this is a phase of business growth that is a major driver of employment and also one which the majority of business owners find the most challenging and difficult, yet for some reason it is largely ignored by the help and advisory bodies out there.

There are in fact two major TRANSITIONS for a growing business, one occurring when the company employs around thirty people and a second when that number increases to around seventy-five. The first of these is, by a very long shot, the hardest. Why? Because this is when the owner needs to put in the first levels of management and change their mindset to one of accepting they must rely on other people because they can't know or do everything themselves.

Let's look at why this stage of TRANSITION (the leap from Level 2 to 3) is one of the most important but complex periods a different way. Here's where the academic language of business growth (infancy, adolescence and maturity) I mentioned back in Chapter 2 can be useful.

Think of the way a human being grows and develops. In infancy we probably go through the greatest period of growth and development we'll ever experience. In fact, a healthy newborn weighing 7lb will be expected to approximately double that weight by six months of age. If this pattern of growth were to continue, many toddlers at age two could weigh in at a hefty 50 kilos or more!

THE LEVELS

If all other aspects of their development (intellectual and emotional) followed their more natural pattern (and so were out of balance with this whopping physical growth) imagine the consequences. I'm picturing the poor parents struggle when dealing with an adult-sized toddler who is having a full blown tantrum because they do not have the emotional maturity or language ability to have a reasoned argument about why they absolutely must have chocolate sprinkles not rainbow sprinkles on their ice-cream!

So, some aspects of our growth and development in our very early years are certainly fast-paced, but is such growth a difficult time?

No, not really. It just happens naturally, we spend our time wholly reacting to things around us (rather than instigating circumstances), and besides there's always someone around to hold our hand.

And then comes puberty! All of a sudden, we get to a stage in life when we're far more aware of ourselves as an individual, feeling quite happy with our place in the world, when BAM, along comes another period of growth that threatens to knock us down a peg or two. Our awareness of the world and of our own feelings makes us vulnerable, we now have to make lots of decisions for ourselves and that guiding hand seems to be disappearing.

It may not be a perfect analogy, but I hope you get my point as I explain that basically something very similar happens in business. Up until Level 2 (the infant stage), the business just seems to grow naturally. It is reacting to circumstances around it, picking up snippets of knowledge and experience along the way and benefiting from some of those helping hands that are in abundance for the start-up.

By reaching Level 2, the business owner is kind of like the child in the top year of primary school – the big fish in the small pond. They are seen by their peers, family and professional advisors as successful but, continuing in the same vein as they always have leads to many of those out-of-balance symptoms that can have a major impact on the long-term health of the business and sometimes the individual too. Basically they are not going to survive 'Big School'.

Making the TRANSITION to Level 3 is therefore a bit like going through the adolescent stage of life. The business owner may be more aware of the challenges around them but has major decisions to face and no clear help to battle through.

The business has effectively outgrown the business owner who has by now become risk averse.

Because of their need to protect their accumulated wealth, ego and reputation, they are neither willing nor able to take chances and find it difficult to put their trust in others.

To get through this biggest period of change, the owner has to get over this!

The only way to further growth is with a change of structure, a change of mindset, a change of people and a change of results. It's the classic principle of cause and effect – you have to look at what is causing difficulty for the business, make the necessary changes to the root cause rather than just treat the symptoms and only then can you expect to see better results. As Marshall Goldsmith so succinctly puts it: "What Got you Here Won't Get You There". (See Further Reading at the end of this book)

Here's the good news: the step change this requires of you, while monumental, does not have to be painful. It's my intention here to be the guiding hand and walk you through the structural and mindset changes that lie ahead. I am going to ask you to look back at the foundations your business was built on and truly examine your way of thinking.

The results will be worth it but in case you don't quite believe that yet and are still wondering whether the hard work is going to pay off, let's take a look at an example of how the real *value* of a business changes during this period of growth.

Imagine a small IT company that was started by an individual who had previously worked as a technician for other companies. The experience of redundancy and a small financial package led him to start his own business and twenty years later he now has fifteen employees. While there are a few key individuals he feels he can rely on, the business itself is heavily reliant on him, the owner, to keep it running.

The owner, however, thinks of his business as his pension. One day soon, he is going to sell it and live a nice life on the profits of the sale.

The problem is that the goodwill the owner has built within the business has very limited commercial value without the owner at the helm.

When he comes to try to enlist a sale, potential purchasers are not exactly queuing up around the corner and those that are interested are looking to minimise their risk. That might mean seeking to buy the business on an 'earn out' basis, thus paying for the business out of future profits with only the minimum advance payment. In addition, they may make conditions of sale that include locking the business owner and key staff into burdensome contracts to protect their position.

This is not what the business owner was looking for at all! If he goes ahead, he will probably end up in the position of receiving very little of the full value of his business while having to continue working for the company where he no longer has control. And, where on earth is his pension going to come from?

Now, let's go back a few years and assume that the business owner had invested the time he needed to develop the structure of his business and change his own way of thinking enough to get through a period of growth. Having made the value held within his business a priority, the business is now a medium-sized company with seventy employees and a fully-fledged management team. As a balanced Level 3 business, it operates without the day-to-day involvement of the owner; this freedom ensures the owner is in a strong negotiating position when it comes to making a sale.

The valuation of a balanced Level 3 business reflects the consistent growth and record of sustainable profits. Serious potential purchasers will be looking at the business as an investment and will be applying a much higher valuation to the goodwill as it is more proven and therefore carries less risk.

Therefore, the need for a lengthy earn out is negated and the owner is in a position to demand a large proportion of the valuation payable on completion of the sale, rather than being equated with on-going profitability. Any unacceptable offers can be easily turned away. Without meaning to be insulting in any way, here's the reason why you should invest time in business growth:

- At Level 2, you have created a job and an income for everyone who works at the company, including you, the owner.

- At Level 3, you have created a business with jobs and income still, but also with a lifestyle of choice for you, the owner.

The business has significant value by itself.

6
SETTING OUT THE STALL

Change doesn't happen overnight and thank goodness for that, because if it did your business would never cope. Perhaps you remember that I first mentioned a process called 'Setting out the Stall' back in Chapter 2.

The one thing I can't stress enough about growing your business is the simple fact that it's going to take some hard work from you, the owner. 'Setting out the Stall' is where you're going to be putting in that hard work – reviewing everything you have done in your business to date, recognising that change is needed to bring about growth and planning for those changes long before they happen or make any kind of impact on the health of your business.

Managing the change and bringing in the resources you need *before* the TRANSITION period (not during or after) is the absolute key to balanced growth.

Setting out the stall to go to the next level starts by questioning all the beliefs we have about our business, checking those beliefs are both true and applicable to the business today and relevant in going forward.

Let's quickly go off piste for a moment to consider our beliefs.

A belief is something that we hold to be true and all of our beliefs put together form a major part of the filter through which we view the world around us. However, when held up to the light, we can find many of our beliefs to be flawed. The interesting thing about our beliefs is that, because we take them as 'truths', we unwittingly find and accept any evidence that backs them up and easily dismiss or ignore anything that presents a contradiction. It's a bit of a self-fulfilling prophecy.

Our beliefs are reinforced by our experience, just as we saw in the example of the bricklaying company in the 'Moment of Clarity' section back in Chapter 3.

When we are setting out the stall we must be prepared to challenge and change our corporate beliefs. That means looking at the beliefs of the business owner and those of the whole company. They will all make an impact on the TRANSITION.

To become more aware of our beliefs and challenge them at all levels, the mantra must be this:

IS IT BASED ON OPINION OR FACT?

Let's put it another way and look at an example:

Imagine a market stallholder who pitches up in a different town each day to sell an array of variously flavoured olives. She has a reliable supplier for her goods, a stream of regular customers and sometimes manages to generate new interest from passers-by.

Then, one day, a bigger pitch becomes available in one of the towns she frequents. It's double the size of her existing pitch, offering our olive lady a great opportunity to expand the business.

Now, does she simply accept her previously held opinion that the olive market is thriving, order greater quantities from her olive supplier and carry on doing exactly what she has done so far? Well, the problem with that is that olives can be a bit of an acquired taste and the fact of the matter could well be that her particular market for olive sales is already at capacity. If she follows this path, it seems likely she will continue to sell the same amount of olives to her regular customers as before while having to pay a higher rate for her pitch and probably ending up with a significant quantity of stock left over at the end of the day. A path towards ruin looms ahead.

To manage the opportunity, what the stallholder has to do is look at all the facts, taking time out to enquire as to what other offerings her customers might like (market research) along with sourcing potential new supplies and closely examining the cost/ profitability ratio. She will in effect be setting out her stall. By planning and managing the change before taking on the bigger pitch, when the time comes she'll have a stall with olives, cheese, a selection of cooking oils and vinaigrettes and so on. Regular customers remain loyal but purchase more items and new custom is attracted to the stall. The owner also now has an assistant in place, enabling her to continue the process of sourcing new supplies while managing busy periods.

I know this is a very literal example of setting out the stall but what I wanted you to understand clearly is the point about planning and preparing for a stage of growth based on facts rather than opinions before it happens.

Let's now look more at how this works through the Levels.

As I've already mentioned, a great many businesses are started with no clear image of the finished project. In fact, from what I've witnessed, the majority of businesses are started to continue the job that the business owner once had working for someone else. The decision to start out on their own is often born out of necessity (e.g. redundancy) or frustration (e.g. they feel they could do better than their former employer). In both cases, the first goal is to replace their former income.

THE LEVELS

As an enterprise grows from Level 0 and the first few employees are recruited, things start to go off balance. The business owner is working exceptionally long hours, often undertaking all the support functions (accounts, invoicing, quotes etc.) after a full day doing what they see as their actual job. They are constantly struggling to keep customers happy whilst juggling cash flow and ensuring their employees are fully occupied. This imbalance continues until their reach the first plateau – Level 1.

The business owner has now replaced or improved on the income they formerly had in employment and, on average, they are employing their own small team of up to about ten people. They have some good loyal customers, sales have grown and the business is starting to tick along nicely. They can now afford to employ some admin staff who help with the daily grind and they have a small team of employees handling the work. Their own immediate pressures of paying the mortgage and putting food on the table have been relieved. For a while, the business owner doesn't have to work all the hours God sends. It's time for a breather.

To put this in a little more perspective, remember that in the UK the vast majority of SMEs (around ninety-three per cent) are operating between Level 0 and Level 1. But, actually, many of the owners of these businesses are doing very little in terms of setting out the stall. This is the growth period undertaken quite intuitively, in reaction to market conditions around them.

In a perfect world, now is the time for the owner to ready the business for the next period of growth... to set out the stall for Level 2. The reality is that, once again, the process here is far more intuitive and reactive than planned and proactive.

The owner continues to beaver away and, along the way acquires more employees, one or two of which demonstrate loyalty and an eagerness to help run the business. Through sheer hard work and perseverance, the business has made it to Level 2 – a new plateau.

After all the hardships endured while increasing the number of employees in the business, the owner suddenly finds things a little easier and enjoys their new found status. Everyone in the business knows what they are doing, there is a core of loyal customers, profits are consistent so the bank is happy and bills are paid on time so suppliers are happy too.

The business is running smoothly at a comfortable size where the owner knows everyone and can keep their finger on the pulse. They can relax a little and be content as it's been worth all the stress and strain. They can even take a well-earned fortnight's holiday and when they return the business is still there.

The reality of the Levels is that it is relatively easy to get to a Level 2 enterprise. The secret is stamina, hard work and determination. Even without putting the thinking time into setting out the stall, with these three ingredients a business owner can achieve much.

But this is where everything changes!

Having reached Level 2 the business owner now has to make the biggest decision of their working life, whether they have the desire and willpower to take their business to Level 3 or not. It's a decision that has to be based on their long-term goal (remember keeping the end in mind) and a real acknowledgement of the implications the TRANSITION could have on the business.

Unfortunately, most owners never take time out to consider these issues. In building up from Level 2 to Level 3, the business and business owner will be exposed to some of the biggest changes they will experience in their entire career. It's a far cry from the entrepreneurial moment they experienced years back and also far from the instinctive growth pattern they have experienced to date.

At some point, as the business continues to grow from Level 2 to Level 3, it will encounter a major TRANSITION in structure, thought process and growth rate. For the unwary and unprepared, this TRANSITION can be fatal or, at best, lead to that scenario we've come across previously – an imbalance with high levels of stress, unachievable time pressures, reduced profitability and cash flow, poor delivery, strained customer relationships and staff morale at rock bottom.

As I mentioned before, this first and hardest TRANSITION period to Level 3 will typically start to occur when the number of employees has grown up to between thirty and fifty, depending on the skills of the business owner and the type of industry they are operating in.

Take note of this right now. If your intention is not to go to Level 3 then the best advice I can give is plan to keep the number of your employees at less than thirty, continue to work hard within your business and enjoy your current lifestyle. But, read on, because some of the strategies for surviving the TRANSITION to Level 3 will hold you in good stead if you want to remain in balance at Level 2.

Assuming you do want to get to Level 3, then well before you reach thirty employees is the time to start setting out the stall.

In the early pages of this book, I spoke of the importance of your role in working through the Levels then applying it to your business by following a process of Stop, Reflect and Review. This is exactly what I want you to do right now. To start setting out your stall, I need you to reflect on the very foundations your business was built upon and to review your end goal.

Think for a moment about the bricklayer

THE LEVELS

scenario we looked at back in Chapter 4. It is common sense that, when starting any building project, someone has to understand the size and nature of the final building they are working on. After all, the first job they have to do is to dig the footings and lay the appropriate foundations in order to support the finished structure. It's a job that has to be done right and to scale.

Wouldn't it be great if we could do that in business? If we could put in the foundations needed to support the finished business right at the very start, surely everything would be plain sailing? But it's just not possible is it? If we attempted to set up a business in this way it would never get off the ground.

In reality, the foundations we start off with in business are generally those aspects we need in place to handle our financial obligations (money in and money out) and meet delivery (the doing of the job itself). Can you imagine what would have happened if, instead of focusing on these things and keeping your nose to the grind, you'd gone about starting your business by putting in place a management team, accounts department, marketing department and more?

So, let's get you started and look at the practical things you can now do to set out your stall for Level 3. Even if you're not yet at Level 2 but are ultimately aiming for Level 3 I still want you to do this!

Step 1: Review your End in Mind

Be very clear and honest with yourself about what you want to achieve and why you want to achieve it. The 'why' is just as important as the question of 'how' you are going to achieve your goal so please take the time to understand it.

Sometimes the answer isn't immediately clear. Your reason why may have been ignored for so long that it no longer feels important or the initial reason for starting your business may have been achieved and your motivation for growth may never have been thought about. If you really struggle with this question, don't give up on it. You may need some external help from a business coach perhaps to clearly identify the reason why you are running a growing business, but believe me there will be a clear reason and there are no rights or wrongs here. You may be in business because you believe passionately about a particular product or it may actually be fuel for your own ego! Whatever it is, as long as you understand your reason why and have your end goal firmly in mind, you can then undertake the next step. (See Chapter 10 for more on this.)

Step 2: Address the Foundations

Up until now, the foundations of your business will most likely have been put in place entirely by you, the business owner. They will have been strong enough to allow your business to grow naturally to around thirty people, a Level 2 business.

To move up a level, you now need to look back at everything you have put in place and address all the shortcomings that will force your business out of balance if left to themselves. We'll be looking at all the components that make up the foundations and build up the structure of your business in Chapter 8, but just have a quick look back at the Levels model in section 5.2 to see what I mean.

With this in mind, here are some of the questions you need to think about now:

Financial & Management Information

- What financial structures are in place to support the business?

- Do you have a system in place that manages accounts and reviews them on at least a monthly basis? Or do you rely on an accountant to give you the news every six months or so?

- Are your management information systems strong enough to identify the facts so that decisions can be made on those rather than opinions?

- Do you understand what is going on in all the different areas of the business?

- Have you achieved clarity about what has happened within your business in the past?

- Have you identified clear trends so that you can have confidence in the future of your business?

Delivery

- What level of service do your customers and the future market you are aiming to supply expect as a minimum? Again, what are the facts rather than the opinions?

- How are you consistently going to exceed that expectation?

Marketing

- What is it that your company actually provides?

- Is this what the market wants, needs or expects of you?

- What drives your customers to buy a product or service from your business as opposed to any one of your competitors? (This is the first step in true market research.)

Time

- At your business (and at home), where is most of your time spent?

- On what tasks do you feel an investment of your time is most important... on the daily doing, on managing the team, on planning for the future?

- How far ahead are you actually preparing for... a month, six months, a year?

Team

- Do you still have many of the same team members now as when you first started out?
- Are team members in current positions because of loyalty or because their knowledge and experience makes them best suited to the job?
- What are the beliefs held by your team? Are they current or outmoded? Are they aligned to your End Goal?
- If you could sack all your current employees today (without fear of tribunal, notice periods or termination payments) who would you re-employ tomorrow?
- Do you employ anyone who knows more about a particular area of your business than you do?

Wow, those last two questions are tricky ones aren't they? But it's finally time to be honest so truly think about them for a moment.

Can you honestly say everyone you employ is the best person for the job? Do you admit to someone knowing more than you do? Have you even dared risk being found out as not being the key to all knowledge by employing such a person?

I warned you that setting out the stall would be a challenge and my challenge here is really to look at all these aspects of your company's structure and start putting things right.

To raise it up the Levels, the structure of your business is going to need an investment of time, money and resources. Whenever I say this, one of the most common things I hear in response is "I can't afford that"! It may come at the suggestion of employing a marketing manager or implementing a new IT system and it seems almost to be a reflex action. The reality is you cannot build an office block on the foundations of a bungalow so think again about where the true value is in your business, look again at your End in Mind and start shaking things up now!

Finally, I want you to take another test.

Take some time reviewing the last three chapters and everything you have learnt so far about the Levels.

Now, truthfully rate your business between Level 0 and 4 for each of the following:

Size (the number of employees/ turnover etc.);

Structure (what kind of foundations, infrastructure and team you have in place);

Mindset (how you as an owner think and lead);

Desire (where you want the business to be in the future).

What we're really asking here is has the business outgrown its foundations, the employees or indeed the way you think?

Put your results for each of the areas in the boxes below.

Size	Structure	Mindset	Desire

Did you get the same number in each box?

If you're anything like the majority of businesses going through a growth period, I'd guess not. But, don't worry, we'll be going over Structure, Mindset and Desire again in chapters 8-10. For now, be assured that these areas can be aligned and setting out the stall is your first step towards achieving this.

7
THE DRIVERS

Before we look further into the structural and mindset changes your business is going to need to make it up the Levels, I want to review the four main forces that, in one way or another, are driving your business right now: Time, Team, Money and Delivery.

We've seen already how these forces can combine to create a balanced growing business and also how they can combine to create stress when they move out of balance. Ultimately we're talking about the make or break factors behind your business. I hope you've got a reasonable understanding of this by now, but just to be sure, let's look at another example.

You may have heard the old Chinese proverb:

"Give a man a fish and you feed him for a day. Teach a man how to fish and you feed him for a lifetime."

It seems like pure common sense, right? But,

come with me on a little journey and we'll take a new look at the meaning.

Imagine you are exploring a jungle and one day you come across a remote tribe living next to a large lake, stocked with huge edible fish. But, incredibly the people of the village are starving. You can practically see the fish jumping out of the water but the villagers have never eaten fish before and simply cannot see the opportunity.

With the priority of avoiding mass starvation in mind, you engineer a fishing rod and tackle, find some bait and, before you know it, there you are – cooking up a nice big catch to feed the tribe. They soon become reliant on you to catch and cook the fish, but remember you're an explorer in this scenario and originally had no intention of staying with some small tribe.

Naturally, you decide to teach the people of the village how to fish for themselves. With your guidance, they soon get the hang of it. The tribe is overwhelmingly happy with the new found skills and so are you. Your job there is done and you can now get back to exploring new areas of the jungle.

But, six months later, you decide to return to the village to see how they are getting on and are horrified to find them starving again.

What's happened? Some of the tribe are sitting exactly where you left them, doing exactly what you showed them to do, but they are not catching any fish.

You quickly realise that the villagers have

chopped down a tree near the lake for firewood to cook the fish, the same tree that most of the fish had previously sheltered under. So, the conditions in the lake have changed a bit but there is still a plentiful supply of fish. They've just moved to a different part of the lake.

So, what is the moral of this story?

Well, isn't it just like the world of business? The business owner starts his business and builds his team but to start off they are fully reliant on the owner to feed them.

In this role, the owner is locked into the business and as soon as they try to move away the business slows. How they use their time is restricted by the lack of experience in the team and so they are bound to the daily doing.

The business owner works very hard to catch the fish and builds up some surplus to enable them to cope with potential problems in the future. He or she is still holding tight to that fishing rod. (Time and Team are both becoming out of balance.)

So, in order to free up the time they need to explore other opportunities, the next stage is to teach the employees the owner's job. It's time to develop the team (show them how to fish) and by doing so, they can now cover the basic operations within the business.

For a while, everything is good. The conditions in the business environment are benign (the lake is plentiful) and the business can now be left in the capable hands of the team. The owner can now use their time differently – to plan further into the future or maybe even take a well-deserved rest.

However, the trading conditions change and here's where the situation is influenced by cause and effect once again. The customers (the fish) are no longer biting and the team doesn't know how to adjust to the new circumstances. They may have been able to deal with a small symptom such as a broken net by a measure of repair but they don't understand the impact of new unchartered actions like the tree being chopped down (the root cause of the change).

What the team is lacking are the vital ingredients of true understanding and adaptability. They've been taught one way to fish, have become skilled using that method but are left confused when things change. They don't understand the new market (the lake), cannot produce the required quota of fish and so any surplus and profits soon disappear (Money and Delivery both go out of balance). The outcome of all of this is that the owner has no other option but to dive right back into the business, using their own knowledge and experience to tackle the new trading conditions.

To help you avoid such a situation, I'm going to show you how you should be addressing each of the driving forces that help to keep your business in balance. But first, here are a few questions I'd like you to think about in relation to your current situation.

Do you understand what is going on in your lake?

How can you build a surplus even in uncertain times?

How do you adapt to make sure you can still find and catch your 'fish' when the market changes?

Could your team do this without you?

7.1 Time

We all know a saying or two about time – 'time flies', 'time is precious', 'time waits for no man' and so on and so on.

In business, I particularly like this saying: "When you spend money you can always make more but when you spend time it's gone forever, so spend your time wisely!"

But the last thing I want to do here is waste your time, banging on about time! Needless to say, as one of the four drivers behind, in front and right in the middle of your business, there are a few points to make.

First of all, let's be clear. There is nothing you can do to create more time for yourself. You, me and the president of the United States will all get through each day in the same way – twenty-four hours at a time! How you use your time is a different matter and what I want you to realise is that, to grow your business, it is up to you to become a better navigator of time.

Ask yourself, how quickly did the last week go by? How fast has the last year gone? If I'm honest, when I ask myself this, I'd say the last week was like a click of the fingers and the last year like a flick of the wrist! Now, I don't want to depress you but let's put that into context and consider how many weeks there are in an average lifetime of say eighty years. My maths brings the total to just over four thousand weeks. Yes, that's right, only four thousand clicks of the fingers. So how important is your time?

So, yes, time *is precious* and time *does fly* but what's important is how you manage your time and set priorities with realistic timescales. The fact is it takes much more than a good wristwatch to do that.

In my own business, I once employed a telemarketer and noticed their effectiveness had deteriorated. I broached the subject and suggested that perhaps she was procrastinating. She said she did not procrastinate but admitted to something we now call 'productive avoidance' – neglecting the things she knew she *should* do but did not want to do while keeping busy doing the things she *liked* doing and so had convinced herself were *necessary*. Remember what we said about beliefs being self-fulfilling? Well, this was a real case of seeing it in action!

We'll come back to how and why this attitude arises again in Chapter 8 but, for now, take a long hard look at your business. What do each of your employees spend their time on and what do they avoid? More importantly, what do you, as the owner, spend most of your time doing or avoiding? If you're at the point where you are largely still holding tight to the fishing rod then seriously it's time to stop. Your business will never grow if you cannot move away from the short-term priorities of dealing with what needs to be done on a daily or weekly basis and are unable to spend time visualising, planning and developing your business and your team for the future.

OK, I'm now sitting down ready and waiting for that reflex action again... the one that goes something along the lines of "I can't afford to waste time dreaming up a future. I have far too many other important things to do" etc, etc, etc. Right, let's look quickly at this idea of the cost of time. Think for a moment about the last time you took a holiday. If you haven't had one recently, use your imagination here and remember holidays really do exist!

So, you took a two-week break away from work – blue seas, snowy mountains or city tours, whatever it was that took your interest. You had a lovely time and when you returned, relaxed and refreshed, the business was still there. Any longer than that and you might have been in trouble, right?

Now, think again about the entire experience. Did you work double-time in the weeks running up to the holiday? Did the phone/ tablet come out every day while you were away to check for signs of crisis? Did you then work double-time again on your return just to catch up? Was there a heap of missed opportunities while you were away? If you tried to calculate the true cost of your holiday (Your time away from the doing), what kind of figure would you come up with?

I don't mean for you to literally sit and work this out on some kind of spreadsheet but what I do want you to do is re-assess the value of your time. Unless you're happy to be still holding that fishing rod (and if you are, you really should have stopped reading this book a long time ago), you have to start looking at developing your team to allow you to turn your priorities to the longer-term development of your business.

It's an investment that will bring much in the way of a return, from financial benefits such as improved cash flow (who wouldn't want that?) to emotional benefits such as a happy owner and a happy team.

So, if we're going to go for any kind of motto about time I'd go for this one:

"And in the end it's not the years in your life that counts, it's the life in your years!"

A. Lincoln

7.2 Team

When you think about your team, who do you think of? All those people you have personally employed to work for you? Do you include others like the accountant that takes care of the finances or your legal counsel that ensures disputes are resolved? And what of your spouse or other family members who keep the home front running while you beaver away at the paperwork each night? Do they count?

We're not going to go into the minefield of domestic/business clashes right now (I think that might be a whole separate book) but do bear in mind that there are many teams within an enterprise, not only those who are right in front of you on the job each day. So, when you start looking at developing your team, make sure your scope stretches a little wider.

Remember our bricklayer again and the problems we realised he was creating for himself by not keeping the end goal in his own mind and in the minds of his advisory team? To properly get into a position where you can work on your business rather than in it and make the most of that investment of your time, what you must do is get every member of your team aligned to your end goal. Only then can you be assured that cash flow and delivery will remain in balance during a period of growth.

We'll be coming back to this again in Chapter 8 but right now I would like you to consider two things about how you develop your team: recruitment and training.

Starting with recruitment, in the early days of a growing business, it is normal for the business owner to be very personally involved in the recruitment process, selecting every member of staff from top to bottom. This has the distinct advantage that there is some consistency in the type of employee working in the business.

Without necessarily knowing it, the business owner is choosing employees that they like and feel they will be able to work with easily and trust in the long run. People naturally like people who are similar to themselves and this intuitive approach probably selects employees with a common set of values. For this very reason, many business owners recruit family members or close friends as their first employees. It feels safe and comfortable to have people they know around them.

Initially there is often a great spirit within the business with motivated employees that really want to help the owner build up the business. As the business grows, these first employees are the ones to take on senior roles but the problem here is that in many of the businesses I've seen, such appointments are based on the perceived loyalty of an employee (who may also be a family member) rather than ability. In the worst cases, a long-standing employee can take precedence over any new recruits despite a lack of skills, education or ability to do the job.

As in so many areas, the ideas and habits

that were needed in the early days of building a successful business can become a hindrance to its future.

In the area of recruitment, such habits can be particularly damaging for the long-term health of the business. Perhaps the business owner is still doing all the hiring and the firing or has handed over some of the responsibility to their senior team as it is assumed that they all have the same standards. But this assumption may not be correct. In fact, to protect their own egos, those already given managerial responsibilities may not be prepared to take on talented people who have greater knowledge or skills than themselves. Their excuse for this – well, "no-one wants a know-it-all around."

The thing is you probably do need some 'know-it-alls' in your business. The recruitment of skilled people with the right talents, knowledge and understanding will enable your business to make the TRANSITION to the next level.

If, when joining your company, a new recruit quickly sees that they will always be viewed as an outsider or that they have little chance of career or personal development, there's only one way this is going to end – with an entirely demotivated team and a kind of cultural cancer that becomes hard to remove and can, in the worst cases, undermine the entire business.

If, however, your recruitment process is firmly

grounded in getting the best talent in place (putting historical loyalties firmly aside), yes you may put a few noses out of joint but the overall benefit for your business will soon become clear. What you'll end up with is an inspired group of individuals working together to achieve a common goal based on a set of solid shared values.

Let's just take a step back quickly though, as I don't want you to think you can never promote someone within the business to a better, more senior position. If you have enough conviction that someone is aligned to the values of your business and understands your end goal, then you don't want to lose them. Even if their skills are not quite up to scratch, they are still a real contender and, with appropriate training, development and support could be a great asset to your business.

As for an investment in training, you are going to have to do this, regardless of whether you promote from within or bring in new recruits. I'm not going to try to tell you where to go for your training as this will obviously be very different for each type of business, but you should be aware of this simple fact: when it comes to training needs, no one is exempt. Yes, that means that you, as the owner, might have to seek some kind of personal development too!

There are many different methods and tools you could use to conduct a training needs analysis for everyone in your team but I prefer to keep things quite simple.

Take a look at Figure 5 below. A growing business needs to make some kind of appraisal of each employee, which takes a measure of their understanding of the end goal. That can then be followed by clear written objectives, which will include training to fill any gaps in knowledge and finally a means of reward. By reward, I don't always mean some kind of monetary bonus. What you are rewarding is an achievement of a learning outcome that leads your business further towards its end goal. Give bonuses if you feel it benefits the culture of your business but think creatively about what your team actually wants – it may be they would be just as happy with a casual Friday' rule or perhaps the opportunity to work from home one day a week.

Fig 5

You may recall that in Chapter 4 I asked you to challenge the way you think about your business because this could actually be the main thing holding it back. Well, the way you view, assess and develop your team is a real indicator of whether your business will make it through a period of growth, in balance or not.

It can take quite a radical change of thinking to move from a standpoint whereby you're setting tasks, communicating on a need-to-know basis, rewarding length of service and motivating via the pay packet towards an entirely different position. One whereby you set goals, practise open communication that covers the 'why' as well as the 'what' and 'how', reward talent and ability and motivate through your infectious enthusiasm and confidence in the future.

7.3 Money

It's the lifeblood of any enterprise and one I'm sure you feel you have the greatest understanding of – money. You've seen your business make a healthy profit last year so, of course, you know what's going on, where the money is going and where it's coming from, right?

Well, it would be great if this was actually the case, but incredibly this is an area in which many business owners just don't have their fingers on the pulse. Many have no system of producing or analysing monthly accounts and the health of the

THE LEVELS

business is largely judged by the current bank balance or level of surplus.

We know already that maintaining a surplus alone is not enough to keep the money aspect of your business in balance. During a period of growth, it can too easily be consumed. Frankly, it's a lack of cash flow (not profits) that can kill a business.

Building long-term sustainable cash flow is one of the vital ingredients in taking your business up the Levels. To achieve this, you must invest in proper financial information and all the elements of your business that will enable you to adapt when it needs to.

There's that word again – investment – and I can imagine once again you're trying to calculate what it's going to cost you! Well, let me answer that. What it will cost is probably a bit of a dip in profits to begin with but what it will bring is long-term sustainable wealth. Remember, you have to set out the stall before you enter a period of growth so the expenditure has to be made up front. The return on that investment will come when you break through that Level 3 barrier.

So, we've already talked about developing your team and skills, an investment that will make your business more aware and able to deal with all the opportunities that come your way. Your team is surely your biggest asset but let's look at what else you need to be thinking of – your physical assets such as property, machinery and infrastructure as well as the less tangible assets such as your brand and marketing.

Let's look at two examples.

Firstly, to enable you to switch from focusing on the short term (the here and now of the bank balance) to a more long-term financial focus (sustainable cash flow), you are very likely to need to improve on the financial information you have available. That might mean boosting your team by employing a financial expert or training up an existing employee but it will almost definitely need an investment in infrastructure too, perhaps involving a whole new IT system to produce the reports you need. It may seem like a big cost, but think about it. If the result is that you now have detailed information that allows you to make the best financial decisions, then that investment will soon prove worthwhile.

Let's now imagine you are setting out a path towards growth that involves quite a significant expansion of your current product range. How do you go about this? Is it a case of finding a bunch of similar products, placing large orders and cracking on with the sales? That would be the absolute opposite of setting out the stall and against everything we've looked at so far! So, to prepare properly for the introduction of a new range, you might need some market research, a test phase, a reassessment of your brand and perhaps some advertising to bring in the required custom. It all has to be planned well in advance and in the best cases, alternative backup plans are thought through too.

I've deliberately kept these two examples quite vague; from within the pages of this book I cannot honestly tell you where to place the focus of your investment. That will depend on all kinds of individual factors about your business – from how old your machinery is to your current attitude to the use of social media. What I can tell you is that you cannot take your business up the Levels by focusing only on your own earned monthly income. Learning to see all expenditure as an investment rather than simply a cost is what will enable your business to achieve a passive income that secures everyone's future and keeps the cash flow... well, flowing!

Before we take a look at the last of the four drivers (Delivery), I want you to take on another task – to stop and review your current assets. Don't forget this is not just about pieces of equipment. You need to look at things like your company logo, website, security systems and much more – basically anything that is involved in achieving a commercial outcome for your business.

Once you've conducted this kind of inventory, select up to ten items and make an honest assessment of whether each of those assets is fit for purpose now and can help take you into a period of growth. Use a scoring system such as 0 for 'not working at all' up to 5 for 'very fit for purpose'. Then pick out maybe four or five other people from your team and ask them to do the same. Try to pick people at various levels, covering different functions within your business.

I'd be willing to bet a considerable amount of money that the scores you get from each person are very different. That may not be a great surprise. Everyone has different opinions and you can't please everyone, right? Well, the point of this task and what I want you to recognise now is that having polarised opinions within a business is an issue that needs to be tackled. If the IT manager thinks that, aside from a few glitches, the IT system is great but the admin team think it's atrocious because it takes them twenty minutes to log on every morning, then all is not well.

It is true that you can't always please everyone in your team but you can keep everyone focused on the end goal and address all the issues that might be blocking that path. That is your key to growth.

It may be wise, at this point, to seek some external advice. As is often the case, what you see as something that has always worked and so doesn't need changing, an outsider will be able to recognise as the very thing that is holding you back. A business coach or mentor could be another investment (of time and money) that proves worthwhile in taking your business forward.

7.4 Delivery

If I had to say only one thing about delivery it would be this:– get it right every time!

We all know the old saying that if someone gets good service they might tell one or two people, whereas if they get bad service they will probably tell at least ten. Well I'm afraid it's all too true and being consistent with your delivery in business is the only way to keep positive relationships with your customers.

When I talk about delivery, I don't just mean the delivery of a physical product in the kind of 'you order something and it turns up' scenario. What I really mean is the delivery of an experience, which comes across through every interaction your business has with your customers. So, from the rapport built up between a salesperson and a particular client to speed of service, it all counts and in fact contributes to the goodwill (or the value) that is held in your business.

Achieving consistency of delivery is what keeps it in balance and, as a result, retains customers. Every single member of your team needs to be thinking about this at all times – how can they make the customers' experience consistently good? Without this kind of common mindset across your business, long-term success moves out of sight.

Let me just illustrate this with a short story: Quite close to home is a great fish and chip shop.

The venue was nicely refurbished a while back and is kept squeaky clean. The food tastes great, the people behind the counter are usually pretty friendly and price-wise it compares with most others in my area. The restaurant has, in fact, won a regional best fish and chips award for the last two years running and proudly displays its accolades.

So, whenever I've had the taste for a nice piece of cod over the last few years this is generally the place I head to. Now, it was always a fairly popular choice and, before the awards were bestowed, I probably waited behind three or four people each time I went there. But, on my last three visits the experience has completely changed. I arrive to a queue sprawling outside the door. The smell of the food is still tempting but, unless I have a spare hour I'm happy to waste, my reaction has been to turn tail and go elsewhere. If I do stick it out, the counter staff now look exhausted and barely have time to say hello before shovelling my order into a bag.

Looking at this from a business viewpoint (rather than from my disappointed taste buds), the issue they are facing is the fact that their increased popularity has led directly to inconsistent delivery.

They've gone into growth without being prepared for the consequences. The outlook as far as I see it is this.

The fish may still taste great but customers will be driven away by the lengthy waiting times and eventually the business will do what so many others have done – level out again at their Level 2 plateau.

Now, I wonder what the owner was thinking upon entering those regional awards? Surely it was part of a plan to grow the business by attracting new customers? So, if that was the case, then that was the time when they should have been setting out the stall – increasing and developing the team, installing bigger fryers, looking at efficiency methods and maybe even moving to larger premises. Do you see that, if they did this now, with a host of dissatisfied customers, it would just be too late?

My point is that, in any business, you and your entire team have to look at every customer experience from their viewpoint. Then, you have to build the infrastructure and processes needed to ensure delivery remains consistent. Do you see customers lining up outside the door as great news for your business or an inconvenience for the customer?

I know that, throughout this entire chapter, I seem to have been urging you to invest in this, that or the other and you may be thinking it all sounds like a bit of a risk. Well, let's be frank here, it is a risk and, while growing your business, everything you change may seem scary at the time. But bear this in mind – happiness itself often means taking risks and, if you're a little bit scared along the way, then that's a good sign. It means you're changing your way of thinking, learning to adapt your priorities, giving value to your business and properly planning for the future.

8
STRUCTURE

Having spoken to hundreds of business owners over the years, I have come across a recurring theme. It goes something like this:

"I used to have a much larger business, employing more people but it was just hassle. In fact, I had a team, the business was thriving and I had a great life but then it started to go wrong so I had to get involved in the business again. I cut it right back and I am now happy. I now employ less people, make a good living and have less hassle. I won't be going bigger again. It's not worth it!"

Before you start thinking maybe it isn't worth it, don't forget what we looked at back in Chapter 5 in terms of the value held within your business. "Less hassle" is usually code for more hard slog by the owner so remember that, by growing your business, you're ultimately aiming for a lifestyle of your choice (the End in Mind) rather than making a living until the pension kicks in.

Apologies to any builders reading here but let's take another look at our bricklayer again. This time, let's assume the bricklayer knows what it is they are going to build. They have the End in Mind. The vision of what the completed building is going to be and its use is totally clear. The plans have been drawn up and so the project begins and the very first stage is to put in the foundations.

Now, this is where our bricklayer is in a unique position. Unlike the majority of business owners, he can put in the foundations that are solid, water tight and sufficient to take the weight of the final structure. With such strong foundations in place, from thereon his job is simply to increase the height.

In business, we know it just isn't possible to replicate this. Cash flow, lack of time and lack of team prevent us from initially putting in the foundations required to take the weight of the finished building.

The harsh reality is that, at Level 1 and 2, hard work and determination are the bywords. The foundations put in place up to this point are quite limited but generally focused on dealing with the finances and controlling delivery.

In these early stages, it's as if the owner has their arms tightly wrapped around these foundations and, because their arms are strong, they work hard and put in long hours. We know already where this leads in periods of growth. At some point the owner's arms are not big enough to carry the height of the building (the sales) and so it starts to wobble.

The point I want you to see is that, to get through the Levels (or at least through the TRANSITION to Level 3), you must avoid the situation where the increased height of your building causes a wobble and the subsequent knee jerk reaction to downsize. At each stage of growth the foundations and structure of the business have to be reinforced to handle the new height.

So, let's look again at the Levels model to see what structural components we need to address to go to the next Level (see Fig 6 below). Bear in mind that, by structure, I mean to cover infrastructure, processes, people, practices and systems within the business. It's much more than the bricks and mortar.

Fig 6

The first elements that make the foundations solid are control over finances and delivery.

These are important because, as we start to increase sales, we want to ensure that the foundations retain the profits and therefore cash. This is where you need to think about the financial structures that currently support your business along with how you are going to consistently meet and exceed customer expectations.

To increase the height further, you then need to get a proper understanding of marketing under your belt. This is what enables you to attract new prospects, make sales and convert them into customers.

With tight financial control, consistency of delivery and superb service your building will seem stable at this point.

To continue up the steps of growth, however, the owner has to begin the process of leveraging themselves out of the business, freeing up their time, delegating to others and bringing in the systems and resources the business needs, including a strong focused team.

It's fairly obvious that the structure a business requires at each level will be different. For instance, the financial system required to support a Level 1 business will not need to be as complex as those required to support a Level 3 business. The same applies to the approach taken to marketing, human resources and all the other structural components that make up any business.

However, the most important question that the owner of a growing business needs to ask is, What is the structure that will be required within the business at the next level? To make it through the TRANSITION, you must put in the structure that can be organically strengthened as the business grows further through the Levels without the need for major costly and disruptive rebuilds.

We know that the major step change for a business is the TRANSITION from Level 2 to Level 3. In the rest of this chapter, we'll look again at how this impacts on the structural elements within a business. Bear in mind though that these are not the only changes you'll need to take on board. In Chapter 9 we will look at the Mindset changes you need to make as the business owner in order to survive the TRANSITION!

As you read through the stages of development involved in terms of both structure and mindset, you'll notice that they all interact; continuously crossing paths and bouncing off each other. Understanding this will be your cornerstone when you come to setting out your own stall.

Let's go over each of these areas in more detail.

8.1 Strong Foundations

Financial & Management Information

When reviewing the financial information required to proceed through a TRANSITION period, the first step is to understand the real value of financial mastery.

I'm still amazed at how many Level 2 businesses and indeed beyond do not produce regular monthly accounts. All too often they rely on their accountants to produce a final set of accounts six months after the year end and, in all honesty, are really only interested in finding out the amount of tax they are going to pay. The health of the business is gauged by the bank balance and very little management information is regularly produced.

The compromise is to maintain a surplus, a large buffer of cash that helps to manage the unexpected but also, in many cases, suffocates any ideas for investment. Where is the process of planning and setting realistic priorities for the business in any of this?

Often the information systems that are run by the business are still those first developed for the business at Level 1 and Level 2.

The business owner believes they have their finger on the pulse and knows what is going on without having to bother with monthly figures, cash flows and all the other boring stuff.

The facts about what is really going on are nowhere in sight and the accounts are simply there to produce invoices, collect cheques and pay the bills and wages.

The information is always backward facing,

telling the business owner what he already knows and so the time and cost put into gathering such information are seen as something of a cumbersome overhead. If you remember, we compared the stages of a business to various boat types back in Chapter 5, well picture this: imagine the captain of a boat is trying to soar forwards without any kind of information about the waters ahead. Meanwhile, the radio controller is busy looking at yesterday's weather report and the navigator is right at the back of the boat, making a nice detailed chart of where they've just sailed.

You cannot make sound business decisions and grow through the Levels without tackling your financial understanding, forecasting and planning.

I know that, for many business owners, the idea of getting to grips with the finances takes them straight back to a time when it was easier to feign sickness than attempt double maths, but this is an absolute necessity and with the right resources it doesn't have to be as painful as it sounds (I promise there are no quadratic equations involved in any of this!).

The language of business is numbers and, just as on an overseas holiday it is helpful to have a basic understanding of the language spoken, a business owner needs to have a good enough grasp on the language of numbers to understand what's going on within their business. Without the numbers, we are once again relying on opinions rather than the facts and that can result in bad decision making about where the priorities for the business should lie.

I am not saying the owner needs to be fluent in that language. They can always hire an interpreter (an accountant) if the conversation becomes too complex or detailed but having no understanding of the language is like being stuck in the middle of Athens without a map. There are road signs everywhere and plenty of people willing to give you directions but if you can't read the words or understand any of the lingo, you have no way of knowing which way to go. With good luck, a little judgement and the use of some slightly mad looking sign language you may well eventually get to your destination but the journey could be a very long and winding road!

As any world travel enthusiast will tell you, if you can grasp the fundamentals of a language you will gain a deeper understanding of the complexities and nuances of the country where it is spoken. Basically, your enjoyment of the trip will be much improved.

So, in setting out the stall to face the TRANSITION from Level 2 to Level 3, the first thing you have to do is put in place strong financial controls and management information that is capable of allowing you to go to the next Level and beyond. Start by making a review of your current information system and take a look at the information it is providing.

There's no time like the present so you can do this right now!

The information systems should be there to allow you and your management team to make informed and timely decisions based on fact rather than opinion. Otherwise it's as if your cruise liner is heading into a thick fog bank with no radar or navigation equipment. It would take a strong or perhaps foolish captain to maintain full speed. So, when you look at the reports your system produces, ask yourself if each piece of information is based on fact or opinion. Opinions are blind spots and tend to lead you down *cul-de-sacs* whereas facts lead to a clear sense of focus and direction, so the more facts the better.

I'm aware that I keep going on about this difference between facts and opinions or beliefs, but it's another area I can't stress the importance of enough. Let me illustrate the point with a quick example of just how much this can impact on a business.

Imagine a large environmental waste contractor. (Size Level 3; Structure Level 1; Mindset Level 1; Desire Level 4)

They operate those huge eight wheel trucks and tankers we see on our roads. The owner's opinion on the business is somewhat clouded by the environmental badge but, in fact, the true nature of the business is a specialist transport company.

As a transport company, one of the major costs is fuel. Therefore fuel usage (i.e. miles per gallon) should be one of the main Key Performance Indicators in the business.

However, as the business has fixed term contracts at favourable rates, the management information has not been reviewed for a considerable length of time. The belief is it would be a waste of time; they've not had to worry about it in the past so there's no need to worry now.

When pushed to find out what the owner thought the fuel consumption of the fleet was, after a little thought, he confidently stated between five and six miles per gallon. (As I said these were big lorries).

Now there is a huge difference between five and six miles per gallon (some twenty per cent) so he agreed to measure the fleet. On getting the facts he was cock a hoop as it came out at 6.5 miles per gallon. The facts had reinforced his belief that all his drivers really cared and were very light with their right foot. Just as he thought, there was no need to worry.

The next step though was to speak to the vehicle manufacturer to seek out the facts around the expected fuel consumption for these types of lorries. The manufacturer stated that, knowing the use of the vehicles, the fuel consumption should be around twelve miles per gallon. Suddenly the businesses owner's beliefs were challenged. From thereon, he focused closer on fuel usage, putting into place strategies that immediately increased the fuel consumption to 8.6 miles per gallon, saving the company £200,000 per year with even further savings to be gained in the future.

OK, let's get back to you and your financial and information management. Once you've reviewed your current system, in most cases it will be time to make some changes. Just make sure that any changes you put in place are flexible enough to grow with the business up to Level 3 and beyond.

Here are some of the main areas to consider:

1. Find a good commercially minded accountant to help you. I have very deliberately placed this at number one because getting the right advice when it comes to the finances seriously cannot be overrated. Take note also that I've said "commercially minded". You need someone who can look out of the front of the boat with you, not someone who can count the number of fish you've just passed. Consider also the commercial value they will bring to your business. If you think this is a cost you cannot afford, think again. The value of good financial forecasting soon overrides the cost of a good advisor.
2. Get an understanding of everything that is driving the profitability, balance sheet and cashflow within the business. What are the

main drivers of your business and how can you leverage your uniqueness? Identify where the value is in your business and how you can measure it. For instance, are you giving any consideration to the value held within your brand and if not, does this mean you're missing out on opportunities to increase prices and raise your margins? There is an old adage that if you can't measure it you can't improve it so make a measure of everything!

3. The balance sheet is a much ignored document within most businesses but ignore it at your peril. An up-to-date balance sheet is your key to understanding very significant financial information about your business – what you own (assets and cash position) and what you owe (debt). It's the only way you can tell if there is real value in your business at any given time and also a means of keeping tight control over the way things will go in the future.

4. It's not the lack of profits that kills a business, it's the lack of cashflow. Growth will produce profits that pass through the balance sheet to yield cashflow, which then funds further growth. It seems a natural cycle, but in reality the profits can get held up (perhaps in debtors, stocks or the belief that a high level of surplus is necessary). Focusing your business on the consistent release of cashflow (now and in the future) is essential to feed the investment

THE LEVELS

required to successfully navigate the TRANSITION from Level 2 to 3 and beyond.

5. A good financial advisor can help you by preparing a cashflow forecast, which should cover at least the next twelve months. Although not immune to environmental changes, such a forecast can forewarn you of upcoming surpluses or shortages and so enable you to make the right decisions in respect of planned investment or perhaps a planned business loan.
6. Set financial priorities and align your whole business and everyone in it to the achievement of those priorities. Use Key Performance Indicators (KPIs) as a way of measuring progress but remember it's nice to know where you have been but much more important to know where you are going. So, make sure your KPIs include a means of measuring forward planning. Use your Financial and Information systems to help you set priorities, focus and align the team and measure outcomes.

What's also important is to get buy in from every member of the team to be held accountable (including yourself). We'll cover much more on this in Chapter 9 but, for now, take note that you should be using KPIs to 'Keep People Informed' not as a stick to beat them (or yourself)!

This is not intended to be an exhaustive list of issues around the financial foundations to look at.

That would form a book in itself but, by addressing these areas, you will at least be better able to read the vital signs of your business and understand the direction you need to take in order to achieve the kind of financial know-how and information needed for growth.

Delivery

Let me repeat something I said in the last chapter: delivery means the total customer experience and, to ensure it is consistent, you have to get it right every time!

Because keeping tight controls over delivery is an essential part of strengthening the foundations of any business, let's just go over a few things you can do to check how you are doing right now and what changes you might consider.

Remember to keep in mind that delivery is not just that final part of our interaction with the customer, the physical delivery of the product or service. Delivery encompasses every experience the customer enjoys from the very first point of contact, which may be a marketing piece, to the aftercare and follow up.

The really important thing to grasp is that the total customer experience should always be in line with or exceed what is promised in your marketing. Look at things from your customers' point of view, not from your own. What are the facts about the delivery your customers experience? Don't rely on what you and your team think.

Rating customer satisfaction levels should be a top priority for any business but it is also something that seems quite difficult to gauge. You often don't hear anything from your clientele unless they are particularly unhappy about something.

So, what can you do to get a better understanding of the customer experience from their viewpoint?

The way I see it, there are three main things you can do quite easily:

1. ASK!

Well, that's really not rocket science but so many businesses get this wrong. Instead of truly wanting to know what the customers are experiencing they send out questionnaires with slanted questions to confirm how great the delivery is so they can tick a few boxes.

So, find and use every means available to truly ask customers about their experience of interacting with your business. That could mean written or online customer surveys, email or telephone conversations, social media interaction or soliciting feedback through your website. Whatever method you choose, make sure you are specific in your line of questioning. Asking someone a vague "How did we do?" is not going to give you any information to work on. So, create a satisfaction scale of say 1-5 and ask questions that tackle specific parts of your delivery e.g. Did you find our salesperson knowledgeable? Was our product delivered within the timescale we quoted?

In any kind of situation where you are soliciting feedback, you should also take the opportunity to understand what your customers expected from your business before coming to you. So, questions that compare expectations with actual experience are great e.g. How long did you expect to wait before being served? How long did it take until you were served on this occasion?

2. LISTEN!

Listen and make changes. The key point of asking your customers is not to do it purely for the sake of list making (of the "we did good at this"/"we did badly at this" kind). To make the TRANSITION up the Levels you need to create action plans on how you can maintain and improve the customer experience through the next period of growth. If, for instance, your business is failing to meet expectations because the sales team is making promises the business can't keep, then you might implement a fresh programme of training, review any target setting processes that might be leading to bad sales tactics, and set a period in which to monitor the team.

3. MONITOR!

Keeping a regular check on all the processes, practices and behaviours your business displays is another way of keeping control over delivery. Consider how everything you do impacts on your customers and, even when things appear to be going well, monitor that impact.

Think back to my local fish and chip shop that I mentioned in Chapter 7. In my view, the business is destined to fall back down a level because they are not monitoring every aspect of the customer experience. They may be meeting expectations when it comes to taste but are failing to monitor the impact of long waiting times.

Again, once you identify what is needed to sustain strong delivery for your business, it is vital to make that change swiftly. You can then put in place standards, protocols and a set of values that your team will buy in to and that will last throughout a period of growth.

8.2 Marketing

"Marketing... that's simple, anyone can do it, right?"

This is the reaction I come across time and time again when I talk to business owners about their marketing needs, so let's just look at this for a moment.

Is it simple? Well, whether you're a software developer or hairdresser you have a product or service to sell, a target audience and the need to find a means of getting information to them about your business. So far that seems a relatively easy concept to grasp.

But, the world of marketing these days is clouded by a whole hoard of jargon – above the line, below the line, branding, e-marketing, social media, the seven Ps, B2B, B2C, CRM, PR, SEO… to name just a few! The simplicity is starting to disappear behind a rather large cloud.

In reality, regardless of the jargon, understanding the best marketing approach to take your business up the Levels comes down to something that sounds simple but can actually be quite complex – getting the right message out to the right people.

Can anyone do it? Well, I'd have to say yes and no here. No, because it requires a considerable amount of expertise to navigate through the complexities of market research, marketing and sales but yes because, regardless of who has marketing in their job description, it is a responsibility of everyone in your organisation. It boils down to communicating what experience the customer can expect. It's about creating a promise.

When you think now of how marketing can help your company rise up through the Levels, I want you to think beyond what may initially come to mind (advertising, brochures, an Internet presence, etc.). Think instead of the message that goes out to customers at all times and how this impacts on your brand and reputation. From the person who answers the phone to who delivers the product, marketing involves everyone.

To be quite clear, this is a subject that goes way beyond the scope of this book. Indeed it will be the subject of a separate book in the series. However, my aim is to guide you through some of the questions you need to ask to start setting out the stall to face the TRANSITION. My advice would be to seek support from a specialist agency or business coach to help you manage this process correctly but, by asking the right questions now, you will be halfway to getting the right help.

So, to simplify the area of marketing a little, I have broken it down into three elements: Market Research, Marketing and Sales. In very basic terms, market research is about identifying the needs of a group, marketing is about communicating with that group and sales is about communicating on a one-to-one basis. The very personal nature of sales means that methods can change radically from one business to the next but in many cases the business owner is the best sales person and it becomes one of those things they find hard to pass down to others in the business.

Because it is so heavily influenced by such varying personal styles, I'm not going to go into lots of detail about sales techniques here. Instead, let's focus on the first two elements (market research and marketing) in turn and see how they will help you.

Market Research

First of all, you should understand that this is the

most important part of the exercise.

I spoke about conducting some kind of analysis with existing customers before but that is only one part of the market research any business owner should be looking at. Proper market research should also take account of your elite customer base, identifying an ideal client and examining the market your business works in.

Put another way, to set out the stall, we need to know that what we have to offer is strong enough and the resultant market is large enough and receptive enough to support the business through the TRANSITION and beyond.

Please, please take the time to consider these areas carefully. The time and thought you put in now will pay you back over and over again in the future.

When market research is not given its true importance, assumed or rushed, the result is that marketing decisions are then based on personal beliefs built up from a lifetime's experience. As we have already seen, sometimes these beliefs can be wrong as they are backed by false or outdated opinions rather than fact.

This is one area of setting out the stall that is definitely not simple! But, the factual information gained from good market research could be crucial to ensuring a business takes the right decisions.

Let's dive in and ask some fundamental questions.

Firstly, what do you truly do?

Your first thought may be this is easy!

Take a moment to write it down and look at your answer carefully. Have you like most people defined the business by the product or service you supply?

Well, here's some news for you – the product or service you supply is not necessary 'what you do'! Confused? Let me explain by taking one of the major international high street brands as an example.

What does Starbucks do? Sells coffee, right? Or… is it in the business of providing a great place to meet up with friends, business contacts etc. whilst having a coffee?

Take a moment and think about why you go to Starbucks or any other particular coffee house.

So, when you come to identifying what your business does, look at what experience you truly provide for your customers.

Secondly, who is your ideal client?

It is a commonly held rule of thumb in business that eighty per cent of sales come from twenty per cent from your clients. Known as the Pareto Law, what this means is that within your existing clientele you probably have a vital few, without which your sales and profit line would drastically fall. If this is the case in your business, get to know these customers as intimately as possible. I don't mean get embroiled into some kind of stalking situation but part of your research should be making it your business to know theirs.

Time for another quick test.

I want you to think about three types of customer: An existing elite customer (one of the twenty per cent who supports the bulk of your sales); an existing non-elite customer; and a new prospect.

For each type, take some time to think about how their behaviour and your interaction with them impacts on the four drivers behind your business. Use the chart below and place a cross if you feel the impact is negative and a tick if you feel the impact is positive.

Customer type	Time	Team	Money	Delivery
Existing (elite)				
Existing (non-elite)				
New prospect				

Who is your ideal client? Well, it may be a combination of various different customer types but the important thing is to always consider what their needs are and how your business can grow while meeting those needs.

Having learned what you need to understand your client base better, the flip side is to gain a better awareness of the market itself – looking at competitors, pricing, the supply/demand situation, segmentation and forthcoming trends. A business owner has to be able to interpret this type of information in a way that shows whether the current market is capable of supporting the business to the next level and enables them to drive the marketing towards that goal.

So, now is the time to think about connecting the marketing with the your End in Mind. I love the concept Seth Godin outlined in his bestselling book *The Dip*, around building your business to be the Best Company in the World. Wow, before you go into meltdown let me explain a little. Think about the impact on your business if it was perceived as the Best in the World.

So my third and final question is this:

What would the Best Company in the World look like?

Let's break this down a little.

Who defines the Best?
Most definitely your ideal customers.
How do we define Company?
Review your answers to my first question here, "What do you truly do?"

Who defines the World?
You do!

It may be the Best in your town or the Best in the County or the Best in… the Universe! It's up to you. Just make sure your definition of the World can support you up the Levels.

Put the book down and ponder these three questions for a while. They may give you a few moments of clarity. If they do, write them down quickly before they fly away!

Marketing

The ways in which you can set about marketing your business are apparently endless. I'm not going to go into every aspect here but I do want you to consider one thing that you can do which, in terms of leading business growth, puts most other marketing techniques to shame. I've mentioned it once already and I've called it "creating a promise".

Put simply, marketing is about communicating your promise to your ideal clients.

Coming back to this idea of 'being the best', this is a distinct advantage when it comes to marketing as everyone is looking for the best option and those perceived to be the best are duly rewarded. Indeed, people's perceptions of what is the best are what underpin any brand. Think for a moment of all the world-class brands and how their market and customers perceive them.

When looking for the best in the world, people focus on what is best for them at the time they are looking, based wholly on their own beliefs and knowledge. The world is also a moveable beast because it only relates to the world that person has access to at any given time.

For instance, if I want an interior designer to revamp my house, I want the person who I perceive is the best in my world because they are recommended by friends, have a great portfolio, charge reasonable prices, live nearby and are available within the next month or so. In business, the global marketplace may seem to be expanding day by day but, for the vast majority of SMEs, the world they operate in is much more of a micro market.

Think about the market in which your business operates in now and see if you can place yourself in it. Are you near the top as the best in business or maybe somewhere in the middle and have settled for being average? If so, it's time to get out of that comfort zone right now and start aiming higher.

Just recognise that becoming the best (for all its advantages) is going to take a long hard climb and only the few will make it to the top. What Seth Godin says is very true – you cannot be the best at everything, so quit trying.

Instead, focus on the areas in which you can be the best and slog it out until you reach the top. What you'll end up with is something that will help keep the four drivers behind your business in balance. By prioritising and focusing time on what you do best within your market and investing in a team that can follow this through, you're basically creating a promise for your customers. Because it is well focused, delivery can be met consistently and your investment soon brings a return in monetary terms.

A well-kept promise is in fact one of the best forms of marketing!

I want to leave you here with a final word about communication – the ways and means by which you send out the message (that promise) about your business. In marketing terms, getting this right is generally about ensuring your message is engaging for your customer base, is relevant to their needs and is highly visible within their world. In other words, there's not a great deal to gain by putting up roadside banners announcing a new gadget for the visually impaired.

When making the TRANSITION from Level 2 to Level 3, business owners have to make a mindset change in their communication tactics. It's the difference between giving out a message that assumes what customers want, saying "this is what we do, come and get it" to one that knows what an ideal client needs and says "here is the answer to your need".

To see how your business is handling its communications, answer these few questions:

- Who will be receiving your message?
- Where do they sit in relation to your business/what type of customer are they?
- What are their interests/needs?

- Does my message reflect this?
- What is their motivation to move to purchase?
- How do they normally receive information about my business and its competitors?
- Is the medium we're using relevant and visible in their world?

You should use questions like this when planning any new aspect of your marketing and communications. It's part of setting out your stall and every time you do this you'll gain a better understanding of your customers, the process will become easier and the step up to the next level will not seem so steep.

8.3 Time

Now you may be thinking "I haven't got time for all this. I'm working all the hours God sends at the moment."

So now is the time to think differently about time. We have looked at it at in some depth in Chapter 7 as one of the drivers of the business but let's look at how we can make a change.

Leverage

You should know, by now, that to make the TRANSITION up to at least Level 3, you have to re-assess the value of your time and start a process of extracting yourself out of the 'doing business' mode by leveraging your time.

Leverage is not my most favourite word but it does exactly describe what is needed – getting more output from the same input. How can you leverage your time and your team's time more effectively?

Firstly, you need to review and improve the effectiveness of your systems and processes that pass on the understanding of your experience. Then it's time to build a strong team and start multiplying everyone's effectiveness.

I'll come back to this in a moment, but first let's take a quick look at one of the biggest thieves of our time that, if not recognised, will delay setting out the stall.

Productive Avoidance

Finding pleasure and enjoyment in our work is something that has great benefits on a personal level for the individual and in terms of effectiveness and productivity for the business.

But, while making work a pleasure is certainly desirable, it's important to note that this doesn't give you license to concentrate only on the things you personally enjoy. No business can run purely on the 'fun' factor. Ignoring the things you should be doing but don't like to do is in fact the emergence of 'productive avoidance', something that I first mentioned when we talked about the way you use your time in Chapter 7.

I'd like you to think seriously about this because I've seen many times how it can gravely affect the way in which a business manages the TRANSITION through the Levels. The answer lies in setting priorities that are based on the value that each task brings and seeking alternative solutions to the achievement of the tasks that may not be the most 'liked' but are necessary for the health of the business.

So, before we go much further let's perform another task. This one might take a while to complete but make the time to do it!

Start by making a list of all the activities you do as the business owner. You should probably do this over a period of at least a week so as to get a proper idea of the entire minutia you may get involved in.

Next, you need to start analysing those tasks. We can do this in two ways: firstly in terms of how much you like or enjoy the particular task (that's the easy bit) and secondly in terms of how much value the activity brings to the business. This might seem trickier but in actual fact it's not that hard to do. For example, suppose a sales order comes in at a value of £5000 and in total you have spent five hours gaining that order, then the value to your business is £1000 per hour or how much you would have to pay someone else to do the task.

Now that you have a 'like' factor and 'value' you can start to place tasks into categories like high value/high like, low value/low like. See Figure 7.

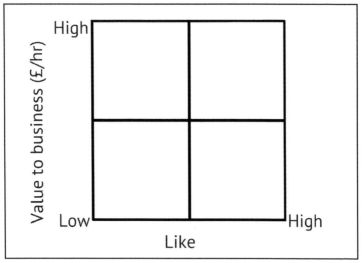

Fig 7

OK, once you've got your list of activities and categorised them, you can use that information to set priorities and reassess where you spend most of your time.

Let me just explain what happens in your mindset with tasks that fall into each of these boxes.

- Low like, Low value – quite honestly, why would you ever do such tasks?
- High like, High value – These jobs routinely get done but, interestingly, they are not always seen as very important because they are perceived as easy. For this reason, they score high in the like factor, probably take less time to complete and so bring in greater value to the business.

- Low like, High value – These are the tasks you really should be doing but tend to avoid wherever possible. You don't enjoy them so, despite their value to the business, a tactic of productive avoidance is deployed. Such tasks go to the bottom of the list while you keep busy elsewhere. (See Fig 8)
- High like, Low value – you're comfortable with these jobs so, even though the value is low, you still get stuck in because it's another way of avoiding those other tasks you enjoy less. The element of productive avoidance influences your decision to place greater priority on these tasks than they perhaps deserve

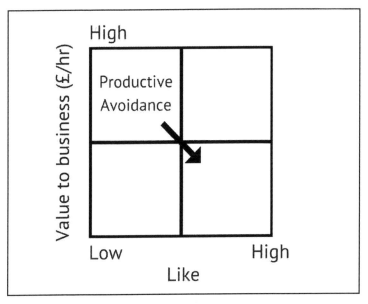

Fig 8

Unintentionally, this results in our default position being to prioritise the high like/low value tasks whilst productively avoiding or undervaluing all other tasks.

Is this a major issue? Well, yes because it probably means the business owner (you) is effectively spending too much time on £6 per hour jobs!

Learning to set priorities on their value (rather than whether you like them or not) is something that will progress your business.

The crux of it all is don't ignore a high value task because you don't enjoy doing it! If you really don't want to do it, find another solution – maybe another member of the team would gladly take it on; perhaps it could be outsourced? Don't forget that if you find you have been productively avoiding then it's likely that everyone else in the company has been doing the same. The only difference lies in the particular tasks performed and that will be defined by their job descriptions!

As an exercise, this is something you can carry out regularly for yourself and with other members of your team. Paying greater heed to the high value tasks practiced by your entire team (rather than allowing your business to avoid them) will bring so many benefits: improving cashflow, allowing for more efficient investment of time and money, ensuring talent is used where it is most effective and so on.

Now, setting out the stall definitely falls into high value – it goes off the scale!

It's <u>your</u> future. It's how you get to <u>your</u> End in Mind. Because of this, I have to warn you not to abdicate setting out the stall to someone else.

<u>It's just too important!</u>

Systems

Systems and processes exist within a business for three very good reasons:

1. To pass on experience, knowledge and understanding to everyone in the company;
2. To enable the business owner to leverage their experience and free up their time;
3. To ensure the customer experience is consistent every time and not dependent on specific individuals.

To set out the stall in this area, some of the first steps could be:

- Conduct an audit of all the systems within your businesses to ensure their robustness and effectiveness. Include HR, contracts, terms and conditions of sale and purchase, transport etc.

- Conduct a spring clean of all the existing systems, processes and activities carried out in the business. In any organisation that has been running for some time there will be mini systems and processes that were set up to sort out an exceptional situation but which are no longer relevant. Apply lean principals to eradicate any waste.

- Review, update or replace your financial and management information systems to give improved visibility and accountability.

- Install sales systems and record processes that ensure the goodwill generated for the business doesn't go home in the cars of particular individuals every night. Review the integrity and security of your databases regularly.

- Look at yourself. Detail all the tasks in the business that you can do better than anyone else. Take some time to work out what it is you do differently and then think about how you can get everyone to replicate this.

- Now look at the whole team. Detail where other employees excel (tested with relevant KPIs). Work out what it is they do differently and systemise and share the practice so it can be replicated.

- Encourage everyone to share their top tips.

This is not intended to be a complete list or indeed indicate what your priorities should be. Every business is different and varies in complexity. If you take only one thing away from this though, I'd like it to be this – **don't make assumptions!** Don't assume everyone else knows what you know and don't assume you know what everyone else knows either. Getting your systems and processes right is about locking in the knowledge and understanding of everyone in your organisation into the business itself.

These can be quite complex tasks and, particularly with auditing and spring-cleaning, it might be a good idea to delegate these to external consultants as they will give you a third-party view. For further help, take a look at the support we offer at Fluid Business Coaching outlined at the end of this book.

8.4 Team

Recruiting and retaining the right talented people is, as we know, fundamental to the success of a business. But, to be a success now, through a period of growth and in the future, a set of talented individuals is not enough.

What's needed is a *team* that is aligned to the culture and common values of the business, as directed by you, the owner.

So, what does that really mean? Well, have you ever wondered what differentiates a winning team from a team that has great potential but never quite makes it?

In sport this is often quite clear. Consider the team of All Stars, a group made up of individuals with amazing levels of talent.

However, when it comes to the big match they don't play together cohesively and are beaten by a team of less talented players who pull together to perform above their perceived skill level. Take a moment and I'm sure you will come up with many examples from rugby, football, cricket and so on.

It's the difference between an All Star Team and a Team of All Stars.

The members of an All Star team work for each other to achieve a common goal, suppressing their own egos to achieve the team goal. Meanwhile, the team of All Stars has individuals playing for their own goals and aiming to massage their own egos.

As a business develops up through the Levels from a micro enterprise to a small business, the pressure to succeed and grow can create a team of All Stars. It often starts with the owner, a talented individual who works hard and excels in many roles and then recruits others who are similar. This may work for a short while but, to truly unlock the potential of the business, the future must be based on building an All Star Team with members that work together.

Let's look at two of the elements that define an All Star team:

✦ THE LEVELS 139

1. **A strong leader that enrolls and inspires their team to achieve a common mission and vision.**

The leader has a mission to achieve and a clear vision of how to set about achieving it. That's something that attracts talented individuals who want to help them on their journey. Each team member may have a different compelling reason for wanting to help but, inspired by the confidence of the leader, they are prepared to emotionally commit to the team success.

All Star teams work tirelessly towards achieving the team goals. They truly commit to the outcome and are prepared to take responsibility for their actions and be held accountable for achieving results.

All Star team members continuously develop themselves and others. A culture of learning, sharing knowledge and mentoring is common and that attracts the best talent that is available at the organisations' salary levels.

All Star team members are prepared to give and receive open and honest feedback.

2. **An All Star team is underpinned by the culture of the business, a set of common values that builds trust between all the team members.**

Interestingly, we assume that our definition of a word, especially a well-used word like 'trust', is the same for everyone. But what is our basis of trust? How do we know that we trust someone?

Let me explain further. We all have our own rules about how we view our world and we tend to put all our interaction with other people through this 'rule filter'. We assume that when we are talking about trust to others we are all viewing it through the same rule filter. But is this really the case?

Think about how our personal rule filter is created. It's something that will have been built up over a great many years, influenced by many different factors – our past experiences, family and society to name a few. It's hardly surprising that we find it so difficult to define a simple word like trust that everyone can agree with. Everyone is coming from a different starting place with a different set of values.

In the business world, this can have massive repercussions.

Imagine being in a situation where the success of a project is dependent on team members doing what they say they are going to do but you know that some are unlikely to deliver. You just don't trust them. What's going to happen to that project?

An All Star team has a kind of implicit trust that comes from a set of common values that are clearly defined and **written down**, not assumed. The values underpin every action and decision, meaning that any issues arising in the business can be openly discussed and resolved to strengthen the team.

Team members are recruited on values first and skills second. Skills can be developed but if they cannot commit to the prevailing culture and values of the business then trust will be quickly undermined.

The successful transition from a team of All Stars to an All Star team is not an easy step to take in business but it is a structural change that helps a business to make it up to Level 3 and further.

We've seen already how misguided loyalty to long-standing employees can hold a company back. Unfortunately, in many cases these individuals can be highly resistant to change and because 'it's always been done like *this*' are unable to switch their thinking to a future where 'it could be done like *that*'.

So, one of the first tasks when considering bringing in fresh talent or developing your existing team is to clearly identify and write down the current culture of the business.

That's not always as easy as it sounds and it may take you some time to pull this off but let's get you started. Have a go right now at writing down the Mission, Vision and Culture of your business. If you're struggling with these concepts at all, let me give you the Star Trek example:

Its mission: to explore strange new worlds, to seek out new life and new civilisations, to boldly go where no man has gone before.

Its vision: to deploy a bold crew and a giant starship into space on an unstoppable journey with every detail recorded along the way.

Its culture: a combination of the warrior ethic (with values of bravery and rivalry) and a sense of righteousness (with values of integrity, loyalty and justice).

Star Trek parallels aside, when you come to writing down your own version, bear in mind that this is a task that shouldn't be taken lightly. It's also something that cannot be delegated; as the business owner you have to do it yourself. If you want to be in a position where you can step outside of the business, you have to develop a culture you personally feel comfortable watching your business operate within. Get it right and you'll have in place the solid foundations on which to build the future. Once this is completed, the next step is to make sure that all employee behaviour is aligned to and driven by the core values of the business. What is the culture of your business when you (the boss) are not there? Ideally it should be the same (whether you are there or not) and that will be the case if everyone has properly bought into the values that you've set down. If you find this is not happening, then for the long-term health of the business this is an issue that needs to be tackled. Tread with care but understand that the outcome will be well worth the angst.

The culture of your business will be the glue that holds everything together.

8.5 Replication

Having addressed the foundations of delivery and finance along with further structural elements of your business in terms of marketing, time and team, there's very little more to say in respect of taking your business even further.

Preparing for and getting each of these elements right is something that will see your business progress right through to Level 3. You'll be at that cruise liner stage where, as the owner, you can confidently step away from the helm and let a new captain take over.

From hereon, the owner no longer has to make dramatic step changes. Instead, it's much more of a case of doing what they've already done in multiplication. In business terms that can mean anything from opening up new divisions of the current business to buying up and improving other companies on the market. In all cases, what happens is simply a case of following the same formula as before – addressing the foundations, creating a customer promise, practicing an expert use of time, developing the All Star team and aligning all to the underlying culture of the business.

9
MINDSET

As the business grows through the Levels, the way the business owner views and thinks about the business and their own role within it needs to change. In short, your mindset has to grow with the business to take on and exploit new challenges as they arise.

Commonly, I have found that the mindset of many owners gets stuck at a level lower than the business' size. This is one of the major factors SMEs suffer as they tackle the TRANSITION, from which many never really recover.

This is actually the time for some soul searching. Are you resisting change to protect your own ego? If so, that could be having a major impact on your business. Change has to come from the top, so get the ego out the way and be prepared to change. I'll cover this in a little more detail at the end of this chapter, but before we look at how mindset impacts on the Levels, let me ask you yet another question!

What is management?

A growing business needs to be successfully managed, but what is management? Try defining it without actually using the word 'manage'. It's not easy, is it?

Well, here's how I see it. Management is about the ability to choose the right (and realistic) PRIORITIES from all the competing priorities for the business; setting a clear path and timescales that leads to the ownership and achievement of those priorities; and aligning everyone on that path. There is, of course, a lot more to it than what is conveyed by this fairly simplistic definition, but bear in mind that the style in which any business owner addresses this issue of priorities (their mindset) is fundamental to its success. I've said it before and here I go again – how the owner thinks about and leads their company is one of the key factors in distinguishing bus-inesses at the different Levels.

Just before we look at the different modes of leadership and the mindset changes required to move up the Levels, I want you to think a bit more about the importance of choosing priorities in a leadership role.

If we look to the worlds of science and nature for a moment, we find there are many basic rules that can be applied – the law of gravity, the law of attraction, the laws of motion and so on. Now, don't panic, I am not going to start conducting a physics lesson here, but I do want you to think about what rules and laws there are that impact on us all in business.

One that makes a daily impression is that 'nature abhors a vacuum', the universal law that empty or unfilled space is unnatural and so there will always be an endeavour to fill the void. OK, so before any physicists out there protest that this is an idiom derived from the ancient philosopher, Aristotle and not a scientific rule defined by Newton, I'm well aware that this is not exactly a universal law. But, in business, it kind of is!

It is in fact a rule very relevant to how a business goes about setting its priorities and the bad news is that there can be many negative outcomes. The good news, however, is that by being aware of its existence, we can work with it to avoid such negative consequences. The even better news is that it applies to all your competitors who may not be aware of its existence, so working with this law in mind will give you a competitive advantage. Let's look at some of the common examples in business.

A. What happens if no one sets a team their priority?

Well, this is where the universal law kicks in straight away. Without guidance from the management of the company, individuals and teams will fill the empty space by setting their own priorities. With everyone singing from a different hymn sheet, there is very little chance of the business achieving whatever outcome the business owner desires.

Identifying and selecting the key priorities is the crucial role of any manager within a business. It ensures the business has focus and avoids the tangled mess that follows when everyone follows their own agenda.

Fig 9

B. How does an individual know what constitutes a good week at work?

It is a natural desire in almost every human being to know that they are being worthwhile, but how is that assessed?

Let me take you back to when you were at school. If, like me, that was a long time ago, this might be a bit of a memory test! Anyway, how did you know you had a good week at school?

When I asked ten individuals this question recently, I pretty much got ten different answers, ranging from getting good grades for homework, making it onto one of the school sports teams or, as one of my colleagues admitted, getting home on time rather than being in detention. Interestingly, all ten had made up their own rules.

Well, exactly the same is going on in many businesses, probably yours included. The definition of a good week for an employee could be the take home pay or it could be keeping out the way of the boss. It could be throwing the odd sickie without being caught or just doing the minimum possible.

The list goes on and on and, although they are not always as negative as the examples above, the problem is the employee, not the company, is setting them all.

The universal law is in operation again and the commercial impact on the business could be huge with lost hours, perceived lack of interest and motivation, poor customer service and so on.

So, the role of the manager is to set priorities for the business and then identify what constitutes a good week for each individual, team, department and indeed the whole company. This is the true role of Key Performance Indicators (KPIs).

In choosing the right KPI for each individual, the manager's role is to make sure they are realistic, achievable and accepted. Great KPIs are those that the individual has the ability to influence, measure and monitor themselves and which have clear timescales.

With KPIs that are aligned to produce the desired outcome for the company, there is no vacuum to be filled and the universal law cannot make a negative impact.

Take a look at Figure 9 and I'll quickly run through how you can put this in place.

Overall I think it's a fairly self-explanatory process to follow. Put your priorities through a reality check filter alongside the individual or team who is to take ownership for the achievement of the task or goal. Ensure you set an appropriate timeframe in which it can be achieved; you can't be reaching for the moon and aiming to get there in a day!

The next step is to put your plans into action, and follow this up by looking carefully at the results, seeking and taking on board feedback from your team. The final part of the process is to follow-through on feedback with new actions and new priorities. If outcomes and suggestions are totally ignored, your team will never be aligned to the new set of priorities.

Priorities are set within businesses at all of the levels and this process can be followed regardless of where you are right now. The difference comes in the scale of the timeframe involved and whether the priories are outcome focused (pro-active) or input focused (re-active). You'll see below that different levels of leadership produce different priorities for the business. A business owner at Level 1 for instance will have priorities that are largely input focused and given a very short timeframe – their thoughts will be about the enquiry that just came in and what needs to be done today to deal with it. In contrast, the owner that has made it through the TRANSITION to Level 3 or above is looking at outcomes they can gain from the market they operate within, perhaps over a period of six or seven years – they are visualising the future. Thinking back to our boat analogies once again, it's the difference between setting sail in the midst of a fog that enables you to see only a few metres in front of the boat and setting out with clear visibility for miles ahead.

It's clear that a business needs direction and confident leadership in order to grow so, without further ado, let's have a closer look at the Levels of Leadership ...

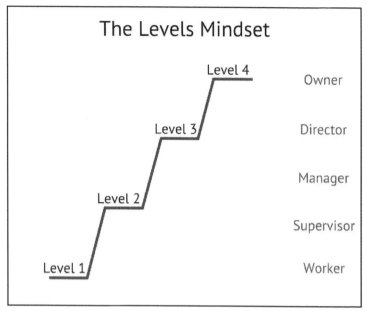

Fig 10

For convenience, I have given each level of leadership a label (Worker, Supervisor etc.) but I should warn you not to take these names too literally (See Figure 10).

I do not mean these names to take on the hierarchical or pride-driven meanings they can have within a single organisation. I simply want you to see how these levels of leadership correlate to the levels of growth and the all-important TRANSITION periods. As you read through, bear in mind that in all cases I am referring to the owner of the business, their traits and underlying mindset.

9.1 The Worker Mindset

Appropriate at Level 0 to 1

At the very base level of starting a business based on their own skills or knowledge, the worker has often only recently emerged from working within another company to become self-employed.

Their main focus is entirely on the job at hand with very short-term priorities that only really look at the next few days (or, in some cases, hours) ahead. Being totally hands-on, they keep their nose to the grindstone and try to deal with as many customers as possible. Time pressures can make delivery inconsistent but they don't have enough trust in anyone else to rely on them. There is no option but to face the feast/famine situation they so often find themselves in.

Despite the stresses that come from not being able to break free of the 'never enough time' trap, ultimately the worker only has to look after themself (and maybe a small group of other 'doers'). So, as long as they can offer some great customer service along the way and maintain an income that gives them a comfortable living, they can easily become content with that.

Here are the key points about the worker's mindset:

- Focused on the daily doing and make long to-do lists for themselves.

- No time to think about the future.
- Cannot trust others (only themselves) to get the job done.
- Have to work hard and put in the hard graft (there is no other way).
- Happy to exchange their time for money as it has to be earned.
- Rely on the monthly or weekly pay cheque.
- Beyond what is required to physically deliver their product or service, all expenditure is viewed as an unnecessary cost.
- Recognise their work falls into a feast/ famine cycle so are always chasing the next order, working longer hours and trying (but often failing) to keep up with delivery.

9.2 The Supervisor Mindset

Appropriate at Level 1-2

As the business grows a little, there comes a time when the owner has to employ others so that they can maintain customer service levels (delivery). Taking on some support staff (administration, accounts etc.) is the first step the supervisor takes to boost the infrastructure of their business.

However, even with a few additional resources in place, the supervisor's priorities remain focused on the short-term aspects of the days ahead, probably looking at the current week and maybe the next week. They may spend some of their time getting others to complete the job in hand but, by and large, they are heavily hands-on and tied into the business. They are the 'best' at what they do, are more skilled and knowledgeable than anyone else and so naturally they continue to make the biggest contribution to the business. Because of this, the supervisor is often unable to take holidays or relax. They do give some great customer service but it's inconsistent and suffers when time pressures arise.

One of the biggest stresses the supervisor faces comes from having to rely on other people to handle some aspects of their business while desperately trying to keep control. This can result in poor communication and support staff being left to set their own priorities. Frustrated that they are not getting the results they were aiming for, the supervisor often ends up claiming they "just can't get the right people" and feeling that they had less aggravation when they were by themselves.

Here are the key points about the supervisor's mindset:

- Focused on getting the job done and giving out long lists of to-dos to staff (allocating tasks rather than setting goals).

- Busy, busy, busy, so no time to check on how

employees are completing their tasks or to seek feedback.

- Works hard and must be seen to be putting in the hard graft (they are probably first in/last out).

- Leads by example but has to keep tight controls over everything because "nobody can do it better" than them.

- Has little trust in others so doesn't require their buy-in and communicates on a need-to-know basis.

- Has workers (not a team) that are wholly motivated via the pay packet.

- Happy to exchange their time for money as it has to be earned.

- Views the bank balance as the key indicator of the health of the business and as long as cashflow is sufficient to fund their lifestyle, that's OK.

- Views all expenditure as a cost, with little thought to investment in the future.

- The main priority is to chase and take every available order.

- Does not need a major change and may in fact not be aiming to be too successful because they don't want to pay more tax!

9.3 The Manager Mindset

Appropriate at Level 2 and the TRANSITION to Level 3

As the business first stabilises at Level 2 and then enters the TRANSITION phase to Level 3, a major mind shift is required by the owner.

The manager realises that what got them and the business to where it is now won't get them any further. They cannot simply work harder and longer to achieve a higher volume of 'doing'. It won't work and so, although it is difficult at first, they come to the understanding that they must rely on others and begin to put in the foundations that allow a strong team to form. They are prepared to start working on themselves and their skills.

Accepting the need to question previously held assumptions, they seek to make decisions based on facts, not opinions. It's time to ready the business for the TRANSITION and building the team. They seek long-term remedies to any diseases (root problems) found within the organisation and structure rather than applying short term fixes to the symptoms that arise within an out-of-balance organisation as it approaches the TRANSITION.

The manager mindset is the first stage of the owner's personal TRANSITION from functional to strategic thinking.

The manager starts to trust key individuals but, because they are so used to doing it all, the temptation to look busy, dive back in and take up the reigns can initially arise at every small problem. However, the manager understands they need to remove themselves from the day-to-day minutia and free up their time so that they can clearly identify the order of priorities for their business.

With that little bit more time available, the focus moves away from the job in hand and towards relatively longer-term planning. Their every-day tasks are now concentrated on building the infrastructure, improving systems and processes that develop a team aligned to the overall business objectives, ensuring cashflow supports profitable growth, and delivering a consistent customer experience.

Here are the key points about the manager's mindset:

- Understands that working on their business is a valuable investment of their time and a major priority.

- More forward looking, focusing on goals and priorities for at least the next six months of the business (but will still roll up their sleeves and get stuck in when the need dictates).

- Realises that they must recruit and develop the right people to take on key tasks.

- Happy to put their trust in others (because they are better qualified) to carry out certain roles in the business without constant interference.

- Sets goals/priorities for the team and seeks feedback to ensure they are achieved.

- Practices open communication, frequently seeking other people's opinions, suggestions and alternative ideas that could benefit the business objectives.

- Enjoys helping others to grow, step up and take responsibility but remains happy to be accountable for results.

- No longer just exchanging time for money but starting to view passive income as desirable (they receive an income from profits).

- Avoids bottlenecks (the negative influences of delivery and cashflow going out of balance) through effective financial data and good use of the balance sheet.

- Views every aspect of the customer experience from the viewpoint of the customer.

9.4 The Director Mindset

Appropriate through the TRANSITION and beyond

At this stage, the business has all the foundations in place to make it a solid Level 3 enterprise with a vision and plan for the future. Having extricated themselves from the day-to-day 'doing', the director uses their time visualising and investing in the future – looking at where the business will be in five, ten or even twenty years' time. Strategic thinking is now second nature. Their whole approach is brimming with success, enthusiasm and confidence in the future, something that attracts, engages and inspires a team that is committed to helping the director achieve their vision.

The director recruits on values first (skills second) and sets clear goals for the team. They communicate why the priorities are important before explaining the what or how and so energise the team to achieve the desirable results. Development is key and, at this stage, the director recognises the need to develop leadership skills in others. They nurture All Star teams and talented people are drawn towards them like a magnet.

Equally important is their change of focus when it comes to sustainable cashflow and a consistent customer experience. The director invests significantly in both their financial forecasting processes and market research. They understand the market, develop and monitor the customer experience and are able to move into a position where, rather than take every order that comes their way, they can choose their ideal (and most profitable) customers.

Here are the key points about the director's mindset:

- Forward looking and focused entirely on the end goal.

- Spends the majority of their time working on the business – brand building, enhancing the goodwill (value) in the business, developing future directors, etc.

- Understands how to invest and receive a return on all expenditure.

- Guides and nurtures the team to provide the environment for growth and an utterly dependable customer experience.

- Delegates naturally, seeks feedback and follows through on all actions.

- Accepts responsibility for their actions and is comfortable with being held accountable for the results.

- Communicates openly about everything, including why the vision is important and how the interaction of cashflow relates to everyone's future.

- Does not accept second best and is prepared to call the behaviour of others rather than ignoring the issue.

- Has financial forecasting in place for at least the next three to five years and receives passive (not earned) income.
- Consistent in all their actions and communications.

9.5 The Owner Mindset

Appropriate at Level 3 and above.

By this stage, the business is generally undergoing a process of replication, repeating what it has done up until now and so continuing to grow through greater volume.

The owner therefore has very much the same focus and mindset as that of the director. They probably have a larger team of 'directors' in place and so the only real difference is one of scale. The cruise ship has become a fleet, the End Goal has probably been reached and so the owner looks even further to the future. Their mindset is totally focused on setting new goals and priorities and then guiding their team of directors towards the achievement of those new priorities.

So, we can see clearly how the mindset of the business owner impacts on the growth of any business.

As you were reading through these different levels of leadership, were you able to identify with any of the particular traits and ways of thinking?

To navigate your way up through the levels I'd hope you can see yourself in at least some of what defines the manager and director but don't worry if you're not there yet.

Recognising that you need to change your way of thinking is the first step.

The second is to start aligning the longer-term priorities for your business to ensure that the team is focused on achieving those priorities so you can successfully navigate the TRANSITION.

9.6 Ego

As I mentioned at the beginning of this chapter, protecting your ego could be impacting on your ability or willingness to make the changes your business needs. So, let's address this right now by asking another of those big questions.

What is your biggest fear?

Let's be clear here. I'm not asking whether you run at the sight of a spider or are scared of heights. What I want you to consider is what your biggest fear in business is.

When asked to think about this, many business owners say it's the fear of failure (or in some cases of too much success). Fear is such a small word but our brain is wired to protect us and so, in the face of fear, we can end up like the proverbial rabbit caught in the glare of a car's headlights – rooted to the spot and destined for a messy end.

The fears we face in business (failure, success, ridicule, criticism, change) may not be ones we can get rid of overnight but, just as I've asked you to give your priorities a reality check, I'd like you to do the same with your fears. They could be a big part of what is holding back your business, but in most cases they are not based on reality.

Let's look at failure, for instance. Failure should not in fact ever be seen as something terrible and final. Most of the very successful people you can think of will admit their route to success has involved a series of failures along the way. Think about it. It's something we say about our children all the time – "they'll only learn by making their own mistakes." Well, the same is true in business. Failure isn't something to be feared; it is something to learn from.

The interesting thing is that the fear of failure often has another underlying cause – the fear of 'being found out'. I'm regularly frustrated when I see business owners sticking to a familiar course of action or failing to bring in fresh talent because of this fear. Their worry is that will be discovered as not the 'knows everything and can do everything' kind of person they are seen to be. But, the fear of being found out stifles change and again has no basis in reality. The owner that successfully grows their business has to accept that they can't know or do everything!

Overcoming and learning from our fears is

ultimately a matter that comes down to judgement and confidence.

Interestingly, when business owners speak to each other with the ego switched off, they are initially shocked to discover that most business owners struggle with similar challenges and common fears. They are no longer alone and can relate to each other in an open and frank way.

Seeking advice from a good business coach or mentor can be a great way of giving your fears the reality check they need, helping you to find solutions that put those fears into context and allowing you to move forward with your business.

10
DESIRE

The American inventor Thomas A Edison, famed as the brainchild of the light bulb, is quoted as saying: "Many of life's failures are people who did not realise how close they were to success when they gave up."

But, why do people give up? What makes one person fall at the first hurdle while another races on to the finish line, regardless of how many hurdles get knocked over along the course?

Well, in business, this is something that goes back to what we talked about in Chapter 4 – keeping the End in Mind. Do you remember I asked you that big question of what it is you want out of life? Take a moment to consider your answer to this again and this time try to be as specific as you can. The more detail you can add the better.

We've spent a considerable amount of time looking at how your business needs to shape up to grow and support the end goal you have in mind, but what I want you to think about now is why do you want it?

The reason why you want a specific outcome in your life and in your business is, in fact, just as important as the actual things you do to get there. It's the strength of that reason why and the emotional attachments that come with it that really explains the Edison quote above. This element of desire is the final factor that can make the difference between those who give up (even though they may be very close to success) and those who persist to the very end.

10.1 The Why

At the time of writing this book, I've just witnessed a euphoric moment in the world of UK sport – Andy Murray's win at the 2013 Wimbledon tournament. Like most of the seventeen million people who tuned in to see Murray take on the No 1 seed, Novak Djokovic, I watched in awe at his display of skill, stamina and nerve. When the final game swung one way, then another, with Murray losing a number of match points, I had to wonder what was going through his mind. What was it that made him keep up the fight, not giving up in the sweltering heat until that final moment of victory?

Of course, both players had the End Goal of winning Wimbledon, but the emotional aspect of why could have made all the difference. For Andy Murray, that may have been a number of things – to break the seventy-seven-year-long history of no British wins at Wimbledon; to prove himself as a serious contender far removed from the wild-haired moody teenager he was once seen as; or even simply to make Mum proud. Whatever it was, it worked, and a nation rejoiced!

So, when looking at your end goal, make the emotional connection. The stronger your desire is, the higher your energy levels will be and that's what will drive your actions and propel you towards your goal, regardless of any obstacles lying in the way.

Think about this right now:

First, get the detailed End Goal in your mind, then identify the reason why you want it and remain focused on it. Now, ask yourself these two questions:

1. On a scale of 0-10, where 10 is ecstatic, 5 is reasonably OK and 0 is close to total despair, how do you think you'll feel when you achieve that goal?

2. Using the same scale, how would you feel if you never achieved it?

If you've scored high for the first question and low for the second then I would say you have a pretty strong reason 'why' already. If not, then it might be time to reconsider your End Goal and adjust the details where necessary until it evolves into something for which you have a greater desire and conviction.

As you try to take your business up through the Levels, having a weak reason why is going to be a recurring stumbling block. In contrast, a strong, compelling reason why is what helps to create the type of leader we came across in Chapter 9, the one that seems to ooze confidence, inspires the commitment of their team and keeps their focus on the future.

However, the why in any given situation can be something of a double-edged sword as for every reason there is to *do* something you'll come across its counterpart – the reason *why not*.

Let's look at this further because what it really comes down to are two very powerful forces that drive our decision making process – the desire to avoid pain and seek pleasure.

Some people talk of there being a fine line between pain and pleasure or that you can find some kind of perfect balance between the two. Well, the issue in life and in business is that things often go out of balance, especially, as we know, during periods of change. You are either being pulled by one force or the other and that's where the strength of your 'why' and 'why not' set in.

The problem is that the desire to avoid pain is, for many people, stronger than the desire for pleasure. This leads to an avoidance of anything that might be perceived as difficult, uncomfortable or cause unnecessary suffering. That's something that can stop you in your tracks and prevent your business from any kind of growth beyond Level 2.

The good news is that by clearly focusing on your reason why you can train your mind to think differently. You can change your view from one where any form of pain or hardship (the reason why not) is dealt with by giving up, to one where such issues are dealt with as something to learn from and keep under control during the journey towards pleasure (the end goal).

Let me make this clearer. We have been into the jungle looking at fishing, we have been out to sea, so let's now go into space!

Take a look at Figure 11 below ...

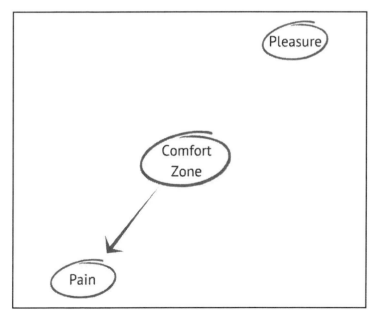

Fig 11

Imagine we have Planet Pain and Planet Pleasure with you and your business orbiting around Planet Pain. You are sufficiently far away from Planet Pain for its gravitational pull not to be strong enough to pull you inwards. There is equilibrium and life is good because all the bills are paid, there's money in the bank and you get to take some nice holidays. You are in the Comfort Zone Orbit!

But, without thinking about it, you just ease off the gas a little and your orbit starts a slow inwards journey of decay towards Planet Pain. At first, you might barely notice it, but suddenly the rate of approach towards Planet Pain increases. Woah, you are going to crash! Luckily, you see the danger in time, get your act together, get back on the controls, put your foot hard down, work really hard, get focused and gradually pull back up until you regain the Comfort Zone Orbit – phew! But beware the cycle can repeat over and over again.

Isn't this exactly what we've seen happen in so many businesses facing the TRANSITION? We know very well that the route towards growth is not plain sailing. When the driving forces go out of balance there can be all kinds of negative consequences – unreliable cashflow, poor delivery, loss of clients and so on. Even when the owner has taken the time to set out the stall before entering a period of growth, there are still very likely to be moments of hardship. Financially, you might face issues beyond your control around fierce competition or bad debts. On a personal level, you might face a moment of doubt somewhere along the line, come under the influence of stress or illness or have to face significant pressures on family and other personal relationships.

Let's face it, the gravitational pull towards pain is, at some point, going to kick in. The instinct to avoid pain is something that will test every business going through growth. The owner may well question whether the pain is all really worth it. But avoiding pain has only one outcome – a move straight back to the business comfort zone. This is how so many businesses end up downsizing back to Level 2.

Now take a look at Figure 12 below.

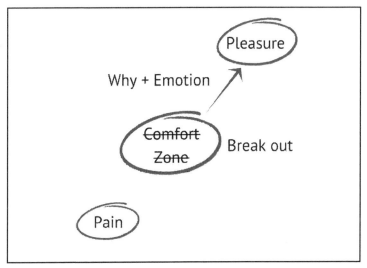

Fig 12

Here again you want to enter a period of growth but in this case you have decided you want to orbit Planet Pleasure (defined by your End in Mind). To get there you will have to build up sufficient momentum to break away from the gravitational pull of Planet Pain and then use the gravitational pull from Planet Pleasure to help you on your journey.

The gravitational pull towards pleasure must be the stronger of the two forces or you and the business will continue to stay in the Comfort Zone Orbit around Planet Pain. What is going to make you break free and stay free of this when the journey ahead is going to be hard and possibly scary?

Well this is exactly why I need you to consider whether your Desire is strong enough. It's time to revisit your why so, if you haven't done so already, write it down now. Get in touch with how you will feel when you achieve your End in Mind. What is that emotion?

The stronger your reason why and the emotional connection to it is, the stronger your desire will be to take on the journey to achieve your end goal. With the conviction that it is all definitely 'worth it', moments of pain can be overcome; getting over those hurdles will be worth it to reach the finishing line.

10.2 Emotional Intelligence

OK, so we can see quite clearly how the emotional connection you have with your end goal can play a key part in taking your business to the next level of success. What's important to recognise is that emotions affect both your leadership role and everyone else your business interacts with.

'Emotional intelligence' is the ability to recognise your own emotions, be aware of what they are telling you and then understand what impact they could have on the people around you. In addition, this is also about the realisation that all the people your business comes into contact with have different personalities, behaviour styles and ways of expressing their emotions. Being able to identify these and respond appropriately has clear advantages.

For external relationships, the use of emotional information has an ever-increasing role in business, supporting the development of effective long-term relationships with suppliers and customers alike. That can affect sales, customer service and marketing and ultimately be used to your advantage in a competitive market place.

Internally, an understanding of your emotional viewpoint and that of others enables you to choose the correct strategy with which to communicate and respond to your team and manage all your internal relationships in a positive way.

Successful businesses are not just the ones who see the opportunities in the marketplace but rather those that can inspire and connect with others. As a business leader, what impact would it make to your business if more of your team could learn to think, act and communicate in a way that builds long-term positive relationships? Imagine if your leadership style and vision-led outlook could not only inspire those around you, but also enable them to enthuse and inspire others.

For many people, the idea of 'work' and 'pleasure' are totally opposed and again there's a balance to be achieved. Well, understanding and using emotional intelligence can turn that idea totally upside down.

Donald Trump once said: "If you're interested in 'balancing' work and pleasure, stop trying… Instead make your work more pleasurable".

Being inspired, enthused, recognised, being listened to – these are the things that make 'work' pleasurable. And, what happens when someone loves their job? They excel at it! They are more productive and creative; they find solutions to problems instead of bemoaning them; and they treat colleagues, clients, suppliers and customers with greater respect and understanding. It's a position that any business owner should aspire to, for it's one that makes the growth journey far easier to navigate.

10.3 Succession

Many years ago, someone said to me *"Time maketh the man"*.

As a young man, I took this to mean that whenever I might be given a new and maybe challenging opportunity, I simply needed to 'do my time' and I'd prove I could handle the situation – eventually.

In my slightly more mature years, I now see a truer meaning to this old saying – that the 'time' element doesn't simply involve the long hard toil. To step up to a new challenge, it has to be an investment in the future, including the time it takes to plan, prepare and mentor.

Let's make this clearer.

As we know, to make the TRANSITION up to at least Level 3, you have to re-assess the value of your time and start a process of leveraging yourself out of the 'doing business' mode. We've seen also that this will probably require an investment in the systems used within your company to ensure you get the right information you need to make decisions. What I'd like to focus on now, however, is the issue of succession and a process of 'stepping up'. That's a step up on your behalf as the owner into the role of working on (rather than in) your business and a step up for someone else to take on a more managerial role. Whether this is someone already within your business or a new recruit, the same conditions apply – they have to show they are ready for that opportunity and so do you.

In his book *The Hero's Farewell* (1988), Jeffrey Sonnenfeld identified four prevailing attitudes at the time of succession. The traits he describes are ones we see over and over again, both in historical leaders and in business. Consider just two of these for a moment.

The General
Generals are forced out of office, but plot their return. They quickly come back out of retirement to save the company. Sometimes there is a plan for succession, but no commitment behind the plan and key areas of understanding are not passed on. The successor is set up to fail.

The Ambassador
Ambassadors leave office gracefully and frequently serve as post-retirement mentors. There is a clear succession plan, which is a process (not an event) to pass on the understanding so that the successor has the best chance of success.

OK, so we're not planning for your retirement quite yet, but if you're going to get into a position where the business doesn't rely on you, it's going to need a succession plan. Are you going to be a General or an Ambassador?

I really hope you said Ambassador right there because that is your route up the Levels and to the lifestyle choices you have in mind. Take note also of the words used here too – that your role as a leader is to pass on understanding, not just knowledge. If you think back to the remote tribe and fishing disasters we used as an example back in Chapter 7, it should be clear that knowledge without understanding is worthless.

To help you plan for this process of stepping up, I'd like you to consider these four questions right now:

1. Am I keeping my reigns on the business and, if so, why?

This is a big question which in most cases relates to your mindset as the owner. It may be you still think you're only 'doing something' by remaining in the thick of things and, without changing that attitude, the dependency of the business on you will remain high. Check out your reasons and see if they are really true.

2. When is the right time to start handing things over?

There are no hard and fast rules here and ultimately this is going to be down to your own judgement. However, for things to work well, the timing has to include scope for careful planning and communication of that plan to all the stakeholders involved.

3. How do I know who is the best person to take over some of my responsibilities?

This is often one of the most difficult things for a business owner to face. It's the old 'I know how to do it best' situation! Try to look at any candidate from a viewpoint based on fact rather than emotion and remember, for you to have a chance of stepping up, you have to give someone else that chance too. This is an area where it may help to seek the opinion of an external independent advisor who will be able to give an emotion-free view.

4. How do we go about the process of handover?

Recognising that it is a process (not a single event) is actually the only thing you need to keep in mind. So, to begin with, think about the environment and the boundaries your business operates within. Initially, whoever takes over some of the 'doing' for you is going to need a safe environment to work in, some tight boundaries and perhaps a period of coaching.

Thinking about each of these questions should help you to see a clear, focused and measured path towards the place where you are investing in the future of your business.

10.4 Finally ...

Most importantly, understanding that why you want something affects what you do and recognising the need to prioritise tasks according to their value over the long term will help you, as the business owner, to break free from the time and mindset limitations that might have been holding you back; taking you and your business through a period of successful growth and into the future. Cruise ship fleet, here we come!

11
STOP, REFLECT AND REVIEW

■ ■ ■ ■ ■ ■ ■ ■ ■ ■

Just before I sign off and wish you well, I want to run through the key points of growing your business once more.

If you've jumped ahead to the back of this book, looking for this summary version, then get yourself right back to the beginning. This isn't your quick route as I'm afraid there are no quick routes to successfully steering your business through the Levels. It does take some work, but be assured it will be worth it!

So, just as a reminder, here are my top ten points to keep in mind when growing your business.

1. Businesses of all sizes go through periods of growth. In the early stages this is handled intuitively through hard work and perseverance, but the TRANSITION from a small- to medium-sized company is definitely the hardest. It's a challenge that many businesses fail to get through but, by understanding the Levels and putting into

practice the guidance offered within this book, you can do it!

2. In business the path of growth is never a smooth straight line to the top and the steps up can be hard work and will most likely bring some periods of hardship. However, difficult times can be managed and downsizing should never be your back-up plan. That's a bit like going into marriage with the divorce papers already lined up, just in case.

3. Your great knowledge or experience (without proper understanding) is not enough. You need to comprehend each experience and be able to pass on that understanding to your team. This will help you to avoid the kind of massive blind spots that stifle the potential of your business or keep you stuck in the daily doing.

4. Ensure your focus is always on the end goal and make sure it's one you have massive conviction and belief in. With this in mind, you'll be able to create a clear vision for your business and then set out the right priorities and values for yourself and every member of your team; ones that are aligned to (and will eventually help you achieve) your end goal.

5. You cannot grow your business on top of the limited foundations it began with. Preparing for growth starts with a process of setting out the stall, looking at every aspect of your

business, addressing shortcomings and putting in place the changes required to support the bigger business you are aiming for.
6. Challenge and change the way you assess, value and prioritise your time so that you work on, not in the business.
7. Get your financial house in order and take time to understand the language of numbers! Use the balance sheet (not the bank balance) as the key indicator of financial health and learn to view expenditure as an investment in the future, not just a cost in the here and now.
8. Strive to develop an All Star team committed to the overriding goals of the business. Recruit on values first (skills second), set in place a strong training and development programme and put your trust in the talent you employ to handle key aspects of your business. Use KPIs to assign goals (not tasks) to monitor progress and achieve buy-in from your team.
9. You cannot be the best at everything so concentrate on what you can excel at and be the best at that. Look at every customer experience from their viewpoint, create a promise that sets the standard your customers should expect and live up to it every time.
10. The path to success is often built upon a series of failures. Whether you ultimately succeed or fail is largely about your willingness to take calculated risks; your ability to overcome

(rather than hide behind) fear; and the strength of the reason why you want to achieve your end goal. A weak reason will lead to any failure being seen as the moment to give up; a strong compelling reason will see it as the moment to learn and move onwards.

Having got this far, right now you may well feel like you're halfway through some kind of very steep hill-walking challenge. Everything you've done in business is laid out on the path behind you and it may be tempting and comforting to look back for it's much easier to slide down a little than tackle the hill. Don't do it!

Everything you *can do* in business (your entire potential) is on that path ahead. There are many opportunities right in front of you and, with the Levels as your guide, you now have everything you need to step forward and upwards. Make a conscious decision to do it and stick to it.

I did it and so did my colleagues at Fluid Business Coaching, the coaching service I now run.

Unfortunately there are a lot of people and organisations out there offering advice to business owners (retired bankers, life coaches, redundant corporate employees and so on) that have never actually experienced all that comes with developing a growing business.

At Fluid Business Coaching we've all been

there and done it.

We understand that a business owner facing the TRANSITION to a medium-sized company has one hell of a mountain to climb.

Whereas many of the advisors are looking down, sending an avalanche of 'words of wisdom' towards the owner, we stand with the owner, look up at the mountain and help them manage the journey up, one step at a time.

In passing on some of the knowledge (and understanding) of those steps, I hope this book has been useful and that the successful growth of your business is very much in sight.

Good luck!

FURTHER HELP
■ ■ ■ ■ ■

The following are just a few further sources of information and advice that you might find helpful when growing your business.

Personal Support:

Fluid Business Coaching

Before I introduce you to what we do at
 Fluid, let me tell you one last story:

About five years ago my wife decided to take part in a 'fun run' of ten kilometres in aid of a national charity. Her starter pack with T-Shirt and fitness plan duly arrived and then, before I knew it, so did mine. Not sure how that happened!

I hadn't run for twenty years but hey I thought I just needed to get fit. Anyway, to cut a long story short, on the day of the race I arrived at the start with both my knees strapped up and after the race I needed two weeks and £250 of physiotherapy to stop me hobbling. You notice I didn't mention my wife who managed to get the job of motivating me as a spectator on the day of the race as she had an "excellent" reason for not taking part!

It's amazing how quickly we forget pain so, when I got an invite to participate the following year, I was totally up for it. I had raised a lot of money the previous year and so I agreed to take part again but this time with a big difference. I wanted to learn how to run.

Right, at this point I can hear you saying "everyone knows how to run". Yes that's true but do they know HOW to run? So, swallowing my pride, I approached a local gym and spoke to one of the personal trainers who agreed to take me on. My beliefs around running were quickly dispelled and we soon rebuilt how I run. Five years later I still enjoy running regularly as well as still competing in the occasional 'fun' run.

Now what's this got to do with Fluid? Do we train people to run? No, but let me explain the purpose of this short story.

Business and indeed going through the Levels is a lot like my running experience. Every business owner knows how to run a business… or do they? Do you? In fact, we often hurt ourselves in business whilst our pride and limiting beliefs stop us asking for help.

At Fluid, we are the equivalent of the gym, but for business. We get you and your business fit for the TRANSITION. We align you, your business and your team to your vision. We help you work out exactly what you truly want to achieve, where you want to go and then we help you get there.

Just like the personal trainer, our professional coaches will not judge you but we will hold you accountable. Sometimes we will stretch you to get you to change; sometimes we will give you very honest feedback.

In fact we'll do whatever it takes to get you to achieve your vision, your End in Mind.

Just like at a gym, one set of exercises or pieces of equipment may not give you the results whereas a different approach provides the breakthrough. At Fluid, we have a team of multi-disciplined business coaches and trainers, an additional wide range of handpicked professionals to call on when needed and numerous tools in our toolbox to get you your breakthrough. We'll be beside you through the TRANSITION.

If you have enjoyed the book and now have a whole range of questions or are intrigued by just how we might be able to help you, then just contact us. Remember every journey starts by taking the first step! You can find all our contact details and lots of other useful resources on our website, such as a free weekly podcast, blogs, downloads and much more.

Simply visit www.fluidbusiness.co.uk.

We look forward to hearing from you soon.

FURTHER READING

Here are a few books that I have found thought provoking:

Seth Godin, *The Dip*, Penguin Group, New York 2007

Jim Collins, *Good to Great*, Collins Business US, 2001

Marshall Goldsmith, *What Got You Here Won't Get you There*, Hyperion New York, 2007

Gay Hendricks, *The Big Leap,* Harper Collins New York, 2009

Ken Blanchard & Spencer Johnson, *The One Minute Manager*, Harper Collins, 1981

Patrick Lencioni, *The Five Dysfunctions of a Team*, Jossey –Bass San Francisco 2002

Verne Harnish, *Mastering the Rockefeller Habits*, Select Books New York, 2002

Martyn Newman, *Emotional Capitalists*, John Wiley & Sons, UK, 2008

To provide readers with further insight into **The Levels Framework**, I launched The Levels Blog: *www.thelevelsblog.com*.

Subscribe to receive regular updates straight to your inbox.

ABOUT THE AUTHOR

Ray Moore

After qualifying as a Management Accountant, Ray followed the traditional career path of working for large corporate businesses within various sectors including food manufacture, engineering and retail.

He took an interesting, some may say risky, career choice to work for a successful serial entrepreneur who became a mentor and allowed Ray to understand his own natural business flair. Over a ten-year collaboration, Ray built, bought and sold many businesses, the group grew to 340 employees and, as Financial Director, he was pivotal in finally selling it on to an FTSE 100 company.

This period saw Ray develop into a commercially-minded businessman who had no desire to return to corporate life so he quickly started his own first business. Over the last twenty five years Ray has successfully set up, built and sold many more businesses. So you could say he has been there, done it, got the t-shirt and a few scars along the way!

Fluid, Ray's current business, was developed from the desire to give business owners down to earth advice based on commercial reality rather than just theory. Bringing together the best business coaches in the area, Fluid is now known for the unique and effective support it offers to business owners and their teams.

Ray's passion lies with family businesses, especially in resolving conflict, managing family employees and succession planning. His personal experience of high growth and rapid change within his own organisations allows him to bring an independent and fresh perspective to these often complex relationships.

Ray currently lives in Chelmsford, Essex with his wife, Jan. They are proud grandparents to seven grandchildren.

Made in the USA
Columbia, SC
28 October 2017